The Real Appalachian America

A Life Spent Teaching Among a Remarkable People

Authored by National Teachers Hall of Fame inductee, award-winning newspaper columnist, and Appalachian native, Ben Talley

Self-published by the author

Dedicated to:
The remarkable people of Southern Highlands
Appalachia, whose everyday lives have deeply
enriched and enlightened my own.

ISBN: 9781717812353

You may contact the author at:
Btalley7@gmail.com

May it do your soul good to know that profits from the sale of
this book go toward funding local endeavors and/or educational
projects for needy local children. To donate, mail to: Planting
Children, P.O. Box 861, Bristol, VA 24203

Table of Contents

Preface

Neither kind nor true have been the words written by too many who have sought to paint portraits of our region. May the reader be assured that the stories contained within these pages are both kind and true to the remarkable people of these Appalachian Mountains.

The following stories about local people and places are of my own recollection and rendition. Some of the names herein have been changed to protect the innocent and, in a few instances, the guilty.

This book contains a very pronounced autobiographical bent. I have written from my own personal experiences, as I feel that is what any author ultimately knows best.

The reader may be a friend from my beloved hometown of Bristol, or a native hailing from our larger Appalachian region ... or simply a fellow citizen of the planet, reading from a faraway neck of the world's woods.

Regardless of your roots, my hopes are that you'll enjoy the following words and thoughts about people from Bristol, a unique mountain town that straddles two states, directly in the heart of Southern Highlands Appalachia.

Each chapter is dedicated to a local community service organization or individual who has given much to our region

Entertaining Angels Unaware

(Dedicated to Sheriff Dave Maples, his loyal staff
of deputies, and the inmates of the Bristol Virginia Jail)

He never knew his Dad. But he did recall a mother. She
died when he was three. All he could remember about his
mother was her laugh … it was long and loud.

He wished he could remember his mother's touch.
Surely she had given him at least one hug, he told me
once, in a brief, unguarded moment. "I know that she
loved me. I can still feel it in my bones. I wish I could
remember just one hug."

But try as he might, night after night, through decades of
drunken stupor, he could never recall his mother's touch.
All he could recall was her laughter.

No small wonder this man called Danny liked to
laugh so much … long and loud.

I taught both a state-sanctioned GED class and an
informal Bible study gathering many a night at the Bristol
Jail for over nearly a quarter of a century. During that time,
I became privileged to come to know thousands of jail
inmates on a personal basis. And like too many of those
men, Danny's self-destructive tendencies, childhood
neglect, and lack of education had sentenced him to a life
of foggy–minded alcohol/drug abuse, eternal
unemployment, and vagabond wanderings.

Danny was well-known around his friends and many
acquaintances for two things:

For one, he had never met a stranger. One of my GED
students described it best, "The first time Danny ever meets
you, he talks to you just like you're family."

No, Danny never met a stranger … and was fantastic at
helping anyone but himself.

Danny once walked two miles across town in a snowstorm just to deliver medicine to someone's elderly mother. Like Danny, this someone didn't own a car, and had no money for a cab. (It bears to mention the fact that Danny was doing this for someone he didn't even know. He just overheard a conversation and offered to help.)

Danny said, "I'll get it to her within thirty minutes. Call and tell her what I look like."

There was something about Danny that made you want to trust him. Even complete strangers trusted him.

An hour later, Danny arrived; cold, wet, and shivering through the min-blizzard, bearing the medicine. Refusing the elderly lady's kind offer to enter for a moment and rest from the snowstorm, he plodded straight back the way he came.

The police found him later on that shivery night, lying unconscious in a ditch by the roadside.

You couldn't blame the officer for thinking Danny was drunk. Every other time he'd been found hugging a ditch, Danny had proven to be vastly inebriated.

So Danny was charged with public intoxication and jailed for the night (an occurrence which likely saved his life more than once over the years).

The second thing people remembered most about Danny was that he was always cussing. He couldn't even be called on to pray in a jail church service, for fear of him letting off a chain of expletives to reach high heaven.

No, Danny wasn't what I'd call a bad sort of a fellow. But like all of us, he had his habits. Cussing just happened to be one of his.

Danny came out for my Bible study gathering one evening, held within the jail library. I was preparing to hold my regular (very informal) volunteer service for the men, when Danny began to tell one of his many hilarious stories. Of course, he was cussing up a blue streak, while taking a pause every little bit to laugh long and loud.

Several of the fellows told him to quit his cussing, at least while church was going on. If it had been anyone other than Danny, they might have even been tempted to let a threat or two fly his way. But, as I noted earlier, everyone couldn't help but like Danny … cussing blue streaks and all.

Something told me to fish around in my pocket. Then I raised up a fistful of one-dollar bills.

"Boys, I've got a proposition for you … if you all can contain your cussing for the rest of this service, I'll buy each one of you a soda tonight. The thing is *nobody* can cuss, not even Danny. Or none of us, including me, will get a soda tonight."

Now down at The Crossbar Hotel, sodas are more valued than money, at least for most. Money wouldn't do the inmates any good where they're at, and most had never stayed attached to any long enough to know what to do with it anyway.

So a cold soda provided great motivation.

You could almost see the men drool. Every one of them immediately said "Let's do it." Except Danny.

"I don't want to lie to you," said Danny. "I can't go two minutes without saying a (blankety-blank) cuss word, so how can I go a whole (blankety-blank-blank) hour?"

I knew Danny's constant cussing was a psychological coping mechanism, just a way of venting his anger back at the world without really hurting anyone. I knew he was at least as good as me inside. More than once I wondered, if my soul had been in Danny's place, would I have fared as well as him?

The way to reach Danny suddenly became clear to me.

"But Danny," I said. "This is not just to help you. It's to help other people too. You're really good at that. I don't know of anybody better."

All the men agreed, because they knew it was true.

I found myself quickly reflecting back on how eloquently another inmate had once put it to me, in his most distinctive, colorful, colloquial manner of speech.

Jeb was older than most inmates, avoided baths like the plague, and grew his hair long and stringy. If you could look past his looks long enough to listen, Jeb would speak to you with a strikingly simple "rode hard and put up wet" wisdom equal to any renegade Old Testament prophet.

"Mr. Talley," observed Jeb, "we all ought to learn to respect everybody that comes our way. You see, the devil might come in here for church service holdin' a Bible and wearin' a big ol' grin. And like it says in Hebrews 13:2, an angel might come in here unaware, because he might be graspin' a bottle and wearin' nothin' but despair. I've got an inklin' that some folks we think is doin' so well ain't hardly doin' no good at all … and some folks we think is almost worthless might be doin' a heap more good than we can see. Yep, we ought to respect everybody . . . 'cause we don't none of us know what a man might be fightin' inside. Only he and God knows that."

But back to Danny . . . who suddenly looked over and shot toward me the biggest of his large arsenal of grins.

"Bartender Ben," said Danny, "you better start takin' our drink orders right now. I ain't gonna cuss no more tonight. It's a done deal."

And it was.

The finest French Chardonnay had nothing on us that night at The Crossbar. We drank one-dollar sodas with the relish of the finest wine connoisseurs in all of France.

I was supposed to have been this man's teacher. It wasn't supposed to be the other way around. After all, what could a homeless, unemployed, uneducated alcoholic teach me?

I learned a lot from this simple, coarse, salt-of-the-earth man ... this soul whose greatest earthly wish was just to be able to remember one hug from his mother.

Not long after our library no-cussin'-soda-celebration, Danny was released again to the local streets.

He was found dead near dawn one morning, curled up in a ditch near one of Bristol's many old train tracks that now lie silent.

It seems Danny had been robbed for a few dollars while he lay drunk, then left all alone to drift in and out of consciousness throughout a long night. The cold had apparently finished him off.

Surely whoever had robbed Danny didn't know him, 'cause if they had, they'd have known to just ask him for money. Everyone who knew Danny knew he would have loaned his last dime to help someone.

By the description given of Danny's dead body, it was not hard for me to tell where his last thoughts had wandered.

The lady who found him was perplexed. Unlike most people found dead in the cold, she noted that his arms were outstretched and his hands wide open, far away from his body.

"I've never seen anything quite like it", said the lady, "It was like he died while trying to give someone a hug."

How to Ask for a Butt Kicking

(Dedicated to places of worship and faith, everywhere)

Little Johnny liked to fight. He was reared that way, out of a sense of honor.

Not everyone understands this "fight culture", but I sought to do so, as best I could. I found that it stems, not from a mean spirit, but from a sense of self-defense, self-survival, and family honor. It's probably easy for many people to "look down" on this culture as barbaric, simply because they don't understand it.

Very early on in my elementary school teaching career, I discovered that as long as these "fight culture" kids and parents felt your intentions were good, you could get by with saying most anything to them – without a fight. I came to look past the surface and found these people to be as "deep-down good" at heart as anyone.

I tried to convince Johnny that he could fight all he wanted, just not at school or on the bus. You can imagine how well my words of wisdom worked on Johnny.

It wasn't hard to raise Johnny's temper. Almost anything would succeed.

But Johnny, it seems, got his ire most worked up over people talking about his Momma.

So … just to see Johnny blow a fuse, that's exactly what many a red-blooded, red-necked American adolescent boy lived to do around Johnny – make fun of Momma.

Finally the principal, another teacher, and I all decided we'd have Johnny and Momma come in for a talk.

Many feared Johnny's Momma, as her wrath was even more widely renowned than Johnny's. It seemed she held a special penchant for being able to beat up men (by which any definition the three of us at the meeting would all be qualified).

But we knew something else about Johnny's Momma; she loved her son dearly.

Contrary to popular belief, virtually every parent I ever met truly loves their children, no matter how misguided one's actions might be.

I always considered it an important part of my mission with parents to find the right buttons to push … and not all parents have the same "right" buttons.

Once the meeting started, it was clear for anyone to see where Johnny got his fiery spirit. Momma came loaded for bear, swearing out oaths left, right, and down the middle. We did our best to calm Momma down a bit before we continued.

Johnny liked me, so I felt led to role play with him in front of Momma.

"Johnny, I'm going to say things about your Momma, and you're going to prove to me that you *can* hold your temper when you really want to."

Johnny smiled and agreed.

So I cut loose.

"Johnny, your Momma is so ugly she fell out of the top of an ugly tree and hit every limb on the way down."

Johnny smiled at me and said, "That don't make me mad, Mr. Talley".

I was afraid to look at Momma . . . but I could hear her breathing. Everyone else in the room must have gone stone dead. I could hear nothing else.

"Johnny, your Momma looks like the south end of a northbound goose."

Johnny smiled even bigger and said again, "That still don't make me mad, Mr. Talley."

So I thought I'd go for the clincher. I knew, Johnny knew, and Johnny's Momma knew, that I didn't really believe my first two statements were true.

So I had to come up with something else really insulting that was derogatory, but still completely untrue. (I knew full well that if my make-fun-of-Momma statements were *actually true*, I'd risk getting mauled by Momma and Johnny on the spot.)

Somehow I was inspired to say, "Johnny, your Momma is so stupid she thinks wearing Army boots makes her look cool."

Suddenly, I caught a clearing of the throat, followed by a horrified glance from my principal.

And my fellow teacher, one of my best friends, wiggled around painfully in his seat and said, "Well, you know, Mr. Talley, Army boots *are* in style now."

This time Johnny didn't smile, but he didn't get mad either. His eyes fell to the floor. Then he cast his gaze in Momma's direction.

I knew where I had to cast my own gaze next.

Glory be! There they be . . . for all the world to see. Momma wore Army boots!

I do believe I could have crawled into a mouse hole, had I seen one.

All I could see was those Army boots. Why hadn't I noticed them before?

Most souls in the room were sharing a near death experience.

Momma was the first to break the silence . . . with a genuinely friendly laugh.

"Mr. Talley, you did it! You tried to make *me* mad, instead of Johnny, to show Johnny I could do it . . . so that he could do it. Now, didn't you?"

I stuttered and stammered around a bit, still unsure whether my life had been reprieved or not.

Momma said, "It worked, Mr. Talley! I didn't get mad at you. Though I've got to admit it, if anybody else had said them words about me, they'd right now be hobblin' around this room with an Army boot plugged up their butt."

All my orifices remained unimpeded that day, thanks to the combination of a deep-down good lady . . . and some even more remarkable good luck.

The Resting Tree

(Dedicated to all who lived and died as slaves in America, once upon a time)

If you listen with the heart of a child and set your spirit right … then you can hear her speak.

She stands now, on Sugar Hollow Park's border, not much more than a couple of football fields from the thousands of cars who daily pass within range of her senses.

Yet, how many of those passersby know what a nearby treasure they ignore?

The Bristol Herald-Courier once did an article on the Resting Tree, stating that I likely had spent more time beneath her outstretched limbs than any living person.

This is possibly true, as I've taken nearly a thousand children to visit her.

It was a snowy day, now twenty-some winters past, when my then toddler son and I first stumbled upon the old slave graveyard she so devotedly shelters.

I've spent many a joyous hour since, gathering the great tree's own children (her infinity of acorns). In turn, I gave her acorns to my students, with the instruction to plant her offspring hither and yon around our good town.

In fact, I've spent enough time in the quiet company of this grand old lady of the forest and field that I feel like I can number her among my many friends.

She's certainly befriended me in many ways.

By my best recollection, she's generously donated countless thousands of her own precious little acorn children for local adoption. Always she gives so freely.

Many are the times I've led a group of young children beneath her canopy. I think she especially likes us to pay visits in the fall, when her own children are newborn.

In autumn, it's not unusual to see her celebrate our visits by casting her brilliantly colored leaves to the wind for children to catch them as they fall. She must love to watch the little ones run.

I tell the children to catch any falling leaf is good luck. But to catch a leaf from the Resting Tree, I say, brings luck for a lifetime.

I have the children gather wildflowers for the few tombstones left from the original slave cemetery. We hold a moment of silence to remember a people who once suffered and wept much here.

"If you're quiet enough," I tell the children, "you can almost hear the crying of families at the funerals once held here."

Indeed, in times past, I understand the Resting Tree was also referred to as the Crying Tree.

I tell them about slavery, that it was our nation's greatest mistake. I ask them to show their utmost respect for the dead long ago laid to rest here. "Many died as children about your age", I say.

The children hardly make a sound as they usher through the narrow path to the Resting Tree's trunk. Usually it takes eight or nine children to wrap themselves completely around the circumference at her base.

The children are always reverent beneath the Resting Tree.

And they seem to sense the evils of slavery.

I take time to pause and make certain they realize no one alive today is to blame for what happened long ago. "All the blame is dead too," I tell them. "But we must not forget," I warn, "or else someday, in some way, it could happen again".

When children observe the Resting Tree, they seem to sense that they are in the presence of a living thing both older and larger than they have ever before seen.

"How old is she?" they always ask.

Well, the Resting Tree is definitely far older than our country. A biologist friend of mine believes she dates her birth back to when only Native Americans roamed this land. In fact, he believes she may have first sprouted from an acorn about the time Columbus first set foot in this New World.

I sometimes hear the Old One speak.

No, the Resting Tree speaks not in words. That would be neither wise nor subtle, both of which she is.

In spring, when her branches burst forth with the buds of a hundred thousand new leaves, she tells of a time when neither a black nor a white man had yet walked below her outstretched arms. She tells me of the first men she knew, red-toned they were, and made use of neither guns nor wheels. She did not like all that they did, but she loved these people.

In summer, when her leaves are soaked with sunlight and her highest branches wave to and fro in the gentle breeze, she tells of a time when black men were owned as property and lived out every moment of their short lives within her sight. She did not like most of this time, though she loved these people. Many are buried beneath her now. Her roots reach out to absorb the nutrients of their remains, so that they may live again as part of her.

In autumn, as her leaves reveal their true colors, she tells of a time when the black men became free, the horse became rarer, and smoke born far away began to pollute the air she breathes. She did not like all of this time, though she loved all those who shared it with her.

In winter, as the days grow short and the great lady sleeps, she still speaks, although in the faintest of whispers. She tells me of her hopes for the people she still knows are passing by. She does not like their addiction to greed over a care for the Earth, a trait she finds to be too common among these new ones . . . but she loves them anyway.

Much larger than horses they ride now, and made of steel, rumbling the earth above her outstretched roots, and poisoning the air ever more.

Desiring much more than they need, she worries that these new ones have forgotten the Earth from which they came.

She wonders aloud in silence, "Will these new ones remember . . . before it's too late?"

The ancient Resting Tree speaks. Do we, the new ones, now listen?

A Christmas Carol, Our Play

(Dedicated to Theatre Bristol, The Barter Theatre, The Paramount Center, and to all those who support the arts in our Appalachian Region)

Used to be, when I taught 3rd grade, the very day we returned from Thanksgiving break, we began practicing our British accents. From that day on, each and every classroom moment until Christmas break would be spent on portraying our own theatrical rendition of A Christmas Carol, by Charles Dickens.

Don't think we stopped doing our three R's either. We immersed every subject, every day, into our classroom play.

I'm sure the original author would chuckle like the Dickens had he been able to see what measure of ribald fun and long-term learning we gathered from his universally beloved story of Ebenezer Scrooge's redemption.

The week prior to Christmas break, we performed our play before the entire school, for a different grade level each day. Parents helped with costumes and scenery, while the children each played an integral part, matching their particular personality traits and talents.

At one point in the play, Scrooge and the Spirit of Christmas Past are both watching Fezziwig, Scrooge's first employer. Fezziwig is rich, but not in the way Scrooge measures wealth. Fezziwig is rich with friends.

The spirit blithely asks Scrooge, "Have you ever seen a richer man?"

There follows a heavy pause of silence, as Scrooge has no answer.

But one of my students, eternally filled with the same constant sense of mirth and mischief as his teacher, stuck his head out from behind one of our props and yelled out toward the audience, in a perfect British accent, "'ow 'bout Bill Gates?" (He even dropped his "h" perfectly.)

Some might say it ruined the point of the play at that moment. But most thought it made the play even better . . . so we kept the line in from then on.

For two years running, my Scrooges were Jewish children, a remarkable brother and sister.

One year, my own son portrayed the narrator, who was no less than Dickens himself.

The local news media came once to do some nice reporting on our play. The children eagerly showed how we infused academic subjects into our play preparations.

For instance, if Scrooge were visited by three spirits a night for three weeks, how many spirits visited Scrooge?

Or, perhaps the children would write a couple of paragraphs describing a character, such as Tiny Tim. Then they'd go back and underline their action verbs.

Several of the children later on told me the play inspired them to try acting in high school. No less than two of those lads and lasses went on to earn some type of part in our world-renowned Barter Theater's various local productions.

Daily we gathered together to read the original book as written by Dickens, of which I bought the little waifs each a copy. Rest assured that a great deal of critical thinking went into the children's paraphrasing of each sentence from Victorian England into words we could more readily understand in present day Appalachian America.

And, all the while, nary a work sheet was brandished toward a child. Yes, we included the three R's . . . but much, so much more.

I fancy that the children would 'ave told you much the same.

Journey of Ten Thousand Souls

(Dedicated to Mount Rogers Regional Adult Education)

Some of the hands that greet me are large enough to make two of mine.
A few tremble slightly and feel surprisingly feeble.
More than a few are viselike in strength.
All portray their own unique mélange of color –
white, black, brown, yellow, red, and/or slightly pink.
Once in a while I even detect a strange hue of blue.
Shaking the hand of another human being, looking them straight in the face, I've come to believe you can catch a glimpse into their soul. I'd rather have this face-to-face handshake any day over a two-page resume. I feel that I can tell more about most people this way.

I count it as a great privilege, and one of my most remarkable human learning experiences, each week as I conduct my tour through the Bristol Virginia Jail cell blocks, wandering along with a deputy, recruiting for my GED class.

From three to seven seconds is all it usually takes … those compellingly brief moments of initial handshake/eye contact. I've found such moments an eternity to conduct a personality read.

For my particular gender, this type of initial contact may be the ultimate friendly greeting.

However, for a handshake to provide me with a true "read" of the individual, we must first make eye contact.

As an inmate approaches the bars we begin to read each other – far faster than any modern man-made super computer.

All his accumulated human ingenuity is quickly processing me: *Is this guy friend or foe? Is he real or fake?*

Does he really want to help me . . . or does he just want to make himself look good?

I've found that it's particularly hard to fool an inmate who has served much time, as he is going to pour his eyes into your soul, searching for answers to all of the above ... whether you want him to or not.

But the clincher is the handshake. In those few approaching seconds, when I "read" each man's face, it seems I instinctually determine the type of shake I should give.

It's always a firm shake. Men appreciate that and would be immediately disappointed with anything else.

Yet the grip must never be so firm as to try to assert superior physical strength. That would be just as bad ... for either one of us.

We seem to immediately sense each other's grip and meet at a pressure point of firmness that we both take to show the utmost respect. Amazing, when you think all this usually takes place, from first eye contact to the handshake release, within less time than it takes to read this paragraph.

Over a quarter of a century of weekly visits, these moments of initial handshake/eye contact have allowed me to peer straight into the souls of some ten thousand men at our local Bristol Jail.

Over the many years and thousands of handshakes, I feel I've learned how to "read" much about each man during this initial greeting.

I'm sure that I don't know exactly how this "reading of souls" can be described in mere words on paper.

However, I've come to believe it's an ability that lies dormant within us all, presently suffocated by our culture's superficial and constant dependence on more modern technological/electronic forms of communication.

Regardless, I'm grateful to have apparently somehow "rediscovered" some of what our ancestors must have known about intimate human communication.

I do know that the men reveal much that they never would in mere words.

When I mention that I teach elementary school by day, some tell me, during that brief encounter of eye contact and hand shake, tales of a terrible childhood.

Some tell me they've given up on life.

Many tell me they'd welcome the chance to better theirs.

A few tell me they distrust me because I'm a teacher.

Almost all tell me they like me because of how much I've shown I trust them, by sticking my arm through the bars - where many could snap it in an instant, if they so chose.

Rarely is any of this information passed on to me in words. Scientists tell us that at least ninety percent of human communication is nonverbal. I'd say they underestimated that percentage.

I've learned that these men, no matter their hand color, their religion, their past, or their future … all share three things in common.

All are human. All hurt. All can be healed in some way.

During an initial greeting I once had a man proclaim aloud to me that he was really Martha Washington, whose dear spirit he believed now lived on in his body.

This man was as steely-eyed and serious as the bars through which we each reached to greet. He went on to tell me that he'd even written some papers on his experiences with George and he wanted me to proofread them later.

(Unfortunately, our current penal system doesn't always succeed in screening and/or treating mental illness as well as it might.)

Another man told me he already knew he could pass the GED test, but that I was probably a racist who thought every black man I met sold drugs. He refused to shake my hand, but only glared at me, prancing ominously back and forth in the cell block, like a caged black panther ready to pounce.

Yet another man told me that he was just "a hillbilly meth maker" who wanted the chance to get out of his cell for a while, but really didn't care about "gettin' no dumb GED".

I called all three out to the library to speak with them.
All three eventually earned their GED.
And all three taught me much about life.

The first man, George, uh, I mean, Martha ... I mean Tony, well, he forever remained convinced of his true identity. But somehow the men in our GED study class all accepted him, just for who he thought he was. Let it be said that we found harmless his unique view on reality.

The second man, Marcus, seemed dead set on carrying around an eternal boulder on his shoulder against everyone missing his particular epidermal pigment.

Marcus once exclaimed, during the course of a conversation, "I wouldn't even drink after a white man!"

Marcus had been taught by everyone in his family to hate Whitey since the day he was born.

After I got to know Marcus, we began to talk a lot. Actually, I listened a lot, because I found that when I talked and gave my opinion, Marcus totally shut down and thought only of what he was going to say next.

Bigotry not only blinds, it also deafens.

Finally, right after he passed his GED exam, Marcus and I got through to each other ... but it wasn't by talking.

It has been my time-honored tradition that each new GED graduate and I celebrate together in the cozy confines of the twelve by twelve foot jail library (where we also have class). I buy each graduate a soda.

Of course, I buy myself one too and drink it right along with them.

Upon due celebration of Marcus' diploma, however, I bought only one soda, a twenty-ounce Dr. Pepper, which Marcus had specifically requested. (It seems the soda machine somehow mysteriously malfunctioned before I could buy one for myself.)

It also seems I somehow couldn't find any cups in the kitchen (which I always could before), so I returned to the library and offered that Marcus and I would share one soda together ... from the same bottle.

"You drink the first half, Marcus," I told him, "I'll drink second, because you're the man who earned the diploma."

Marcus picked up the bottle and raised it toward his lips ... then he hesitated slightly. He proceeded to watch me with great interest for a moment. Should the slightest hint of repulsion arise from within my soul, there was no doubt this side of heaven he would catch it.

Then Marcus did an amazing thing. He handed me the bottle and said, "Mr. Talley, you do the honors. You drink half of it first. I'll follow up."

So I did.

Marcus then proceeded to drink the remainder of the soda with full gusto. Then he slowly laid down the empty bottle.

For I'm not sure how long, neither one of us spoke. Words were not necessary and would only have spoiled the moment.

We did smile and laugh a bit. But we said nothing for quite a while.

It was the last time I ever saw Marcus. He was delivered to federal prison the next day.

Was I able to sway this fellow soul from his imbedded hatred of certain superficial skin colors?

I don't really know, but I do know this - I learned a lot from Marcus.

I learned never to give up on anyone, not even those who portray a visage of hate.

There's always a reason behind why someone is the way they are ... even if our own vision is so blurred or hindered that we cannot see the reason as clearly as we might like.

We are all potentially fallible and given the same unfortunate initial conditions as others, we might very well find ourselves equally prone to humanity's deepest failures.

The third man, the hillbilly meth maker, wound up being one of my best students ever. He told me, as have so many over the years, "I always thought I didn't like to learn. But I found out it was school that I didn't like, not learnin'. I really like learnin', just for the sake of it".

Here at The Crossbar Hotel, Luke found out he had a brain after all. In fact, this young man went on to attain nearly a perfect score on his final GED exam. Upon his release, he eventually set up his own carpentry business, gradually earning the trust of many a hillbilly neighbor back on his ridge of the mountains.

. . .

Indeed, I've learned much from my journey into ten thousand souls.

I've learned to refrain from ever looking at a fellow man and whispering, "I would never, not in a million years, be like that."

And I've learned that I should never sanctimoniously announce, "There, but for the grace of God, go I."

When coming upon a fallen brother or sister, I've come to terms that my wisest words might be these: "There am I. How can I help myself?"

Bedazzled by Butterflies

(Dedicated to the Department of Social Services
and Child Protective Services)

The intoxicating elegance of a butterfly enraptures our senses. It's easy to forget that this creature spends most of its waking days on this sphere as a relatively unappealing mortal ... an unseemly caterpillar.

. . .

One day, one of the kindest teachers I ever knew called me up from another school. She spoke in a ghostly tone, "Billy is going to be in your class tomorrow."

This dear lady couldn't have uttered those words with more horror if Billy had been the devil himself.

"Tie everything down in your room," she advised.

"And don't keep any sharp objects handy. He likes to draw pictures of teachers' eyes being stabbed out."

"Is he really that bad?" I asked.

She grew deadly silent for a moment and said, "He's the meanest kid who ever lived."

Well, I'd seen a lot of those.

Like many of the men I teach at the jail, Billy was early on identified as ADHD, LD, and ED (Attention Deficit Hyperactivity Disorder, Learning Disabled, and Emotionally Disturbed).

As the writer of the biblical book of Isaiah noted wisely long ago, "Can the leopard change his spots?"

I think it more practical (and much less fretful) to meet people where they're at, perceived "spots and all". Experience has taught me that my trying to change who people are is an exercise in futility. Ultimately, people can only change themselves, if at all. And maybe it's best they stay who they are. We don't know everything in The Great Scheme of Things, much as we like to think we do.

Oh, sure, we teachers and parents can artificially alter behavior for a brief while - especially if we become adept, as many with power tend to do, at using both fear and guilt as our primary methods of control.

There is something else, however, that I've seen the best teachers and finest parents do – *teach others how to change themselves.*

I knew that pouring on the fear and guilt would have no effect on Billy.

I also knew, with all that had already happened in the life of this pitiful and violent young soul, that it was not highly likely I would succeed in teaching him how to maintain long-term control of his behavior, either.

But that Light within kept whispering to me in a still, small voice … so I was at least going to try my best.

Billy already had three strikes against him, so to speak.

Billy's first strike: due to his not caring about school, lack of guidance at home, and excessive absences, he was already three years behind in reading – a virtual impossibility to make up.

And success in *every* academic course, including math, depends to a very large degree on a child's reading level.

Billy's second strike: he was a couple or three years older than most of his classmates – a fact that too often dooms children to social failure.

Overwhelmingly, children in Billy's predicament – of extremely advanced physical age for their grade and significantly below grade level reading skills – simply drop out as soon as they can. I can see why.

Billy's third strike was his home life.

His Dad was incarcerated and hardly knew he existed.

His Mom had a substance abuse problem and placed no value whatsoever on Billy's education.

She might see that he had some food to eat at night . . . but only on her good evenings, which were coming less and less often.

So Billy had struck out … already … and he was only ten years old.

This doesn't mean that public schools had given up on him. It just means that, realistically, school was no longer "for him". I had to face this fact to help him at all.

At this point, long division and sentence syntax were of no interest to Billy, nor would they likely ever be again.

And for those who haven't taught in public schools recently, please don't think that Billy stood out so much like a sore thumb in my classroom. On the contrary, at any given time, way too many of my students have led at least halfway similar lives.

Indeed, from my viewpoint in the public-school classroom, the fraternal twin children of Ignorance and Poverty now appear to be coming at us in ever-increasing droves.

So did Billy eventually become a success in the eyes of the world?

Well, he eventually became labeled a juvenile delinquent, dropped out of high school, sold illegal drugs, spent more than one stint in prison, lived off taxes his entire adult life, never held an honest job, fathered several illegitimate children, and stayed drunk a large portion of his waking life every chance he got. I have little doubt he hurled anger and/or disgust toward most souls who came his way.

Yet I know of at least one thing that Billy did in his life that was good, totally of his own choice.

Billy chose not to kill a spider when he could have.

On Billy's first Nature hike with me, I found him mumbling to himself (as Billy often did). He was on a mission. "I'm gonna find me a spider and kill it!"

So I asked him, "Billy, why do you kill spiders?"

"Because spiders ain't no good! I hate spiders. I kill every spider I find."

So I explained to Billy, "Because of spiders, we humans can live on Earth without the constant disease and plagues that would result from an overpopulation of insects. Many more diseases and plagues would for certain occur … if not for spiders. They are really very good for us."

Billy paused, squinched up his face, and said, "But I always thought that spiders ain't good for nothin'."

"Billy, the only reason most people don't like spiders is because they don't understand them. Spiders just do what they do, as best they can do it. To people who don't know better, I can see why they seem to be bad. But they're really good for the whole Earth."

For some reason Billy "got it".

"Wow, spiders are cool!" he exclaimed. Billy stood even more wide-eyed than most kids when they "get it" – that nothing is meaningless and that nothing is insignificant.

The next time I saw Billy find a spider on a Nature hike with me, he just watched it in awe.

"I'm gonna let it live," he mumbled. It's just doin' all it knows how to do … kinda like me."

If I hadn't been crouched down close to him, I'd never have heard his gracious words.

And I would have missed one of the most profound moments of my life.

Those familiar with The Butterfly Effect know it as a wonderful example of the interconnectedness of all things.

There exist many apt analogies, but one goes something like this: because a single butterfly chooses to flap its wings just one more time today in China, then, by a wondrous web of cause and effect, it leads to a thunderstorm halfway around the world next week, in Central Park.

While the butterfly does not "cause" the thunderstorm in the sense of providing enough energy, it does "cause" it in the sense that the one extra flap of its wings is an essential part of the initial conditions ultimately resulting in a faraway thunderstorm, and without that one extra flap ... that particular thunderstorm would never have existed.

The crux of the matter is this: even seemingly insignificant events lead to profound consequences ... if only we could see the "Big Picture".

In short, nothing that ever happens is insignificant. It only appears to be so to us, due solely to our extremely limited frame of reference in the physical world.

Many wonderful (and, sadly, not widely known) discoveries from laboratory experiments within the field of quantum physics appear to point to the staggering revelation that our every single action and thought changes everything ... forever.

. . .

Was Billy's life worthwhile?

Many would say "No". They would say his life ultimately proved only to be a constant and hopeless drain on our society. Many would say that the world (strictly statistically speaking) would be better off had he never even lived.

Who knows?

Maybe Billy's single act of saving a spider led to some wondrous universal change, to which any member of our species is simply too nearsighted in our present incarnation to behold.

Who knows?

I do know that I continue to be bedazzled by butterflies. Whenever I see one you'll find me watching it until it disappears completely from sight.

I especially enjoy watching for that very last flap.

Greatness

(Dedicated to Wellmont Hospice House, in honor of my dear uncle
and true friend, Charles J. Lowry, Sr. "Charlie" twice volunteered to
serve his country in the Marines. He was instrumental in initially
organizing and serving on the boards of the Haven of Rest Rescue
Mission, the Boys and Girls Club, and countless other local civic and
church organizations. Taught early the value of hard work, Charlie
became a multi-millionaire businessman. However, he gave much of
his wealth, time, and endless energy toward helping the poor learn to
help themselves. As Bristol's most renowned real estate developer, he
built more houses on either side of town than anyone. Those houses
still give homes to thousands of Bristol families even today. I wrote
the following words while spending an entire night by Charlie's
bedside, as he lay dying.)

So busy once,
And full of life.

He was born of that generation called Great.
A Marine, he proved himself for God and country,
Keeping a frenzied pace.
Honor, prestige, and valor,
These three he built on every hour.
Nothing ever seemed to get in his way.
But the years . . . so quickly they came and went.
His youth wilted by age,
Vanished away like smoke on the wind.
Love, Compassion, and Forgiveness -
They're all that stand, so near the end.
"These things are all that matters!" He
shouts to us now . . . in silence …
from a hospice bed.
Oh, if only we would listen.
"These three, alone, are true Greatness."

But . . . we're so busy now,
And full of life.

Holy Water

(Dedicated to the Good News Jail and Prison Ministry)

I came into the jail one night to hold an informal Bible study service for the inmates. (For many years I served as a proud volunteer for the Good News Jail and Prison Ministry, in addition to my work as GED instructor.)

Evidently, inmate Jimmy wanted to commence the service before I arrived . . .

As soon as I walked in the back door of the jail, the deputies on shift motioned me over to the control center, where I could view a video camera of one of the cell blocks. The deputies were laughing so hard they did good to walk, let alone talk.

Finally, a deputy spit out the following words between chortles, "You won't need to have church tonight, Ben. They're already (guffaw) having a service back in seven block!"

If it's true that a picture speaks a thousand words … then a good video might be worth ten thousand.

I watched as inmate Jimmy stood on a crate in seven block, slinging his arms mightily through the air, joyfully singing the old Southern Baptist hymn, "There's Power in the Blood."

The other inmates could be seen staggering around the cell, immune to every care in the world, and singing cheerily along. (I somewhat hesitate to proclaim all I heard as "singing". Some of the inmates sounded more as if they were touched by the Spirit and sought to vocalize their exuberance in an "unknown tongue".)

Each time the "choir" approached the end of a verse, Preacher Jimmy's gyrations would nearly wobble him off his crate, uh … I mean pulpit.

I quote straight from the Book of Incarcerations, chapter two, verse twelve: "And behold, I say unto thee, Brother Jimmy, should thou wavereth or faltereth the slightest bit, many a flailing hand of thy flock awaiteth faithfully alongside, ready to proppeth thee back onto thy pulpit."

It began to dawn on me that the Seven Block Disciples were privy to something not customarily served to the inmates at the jail. They were into "the Spirit" alright ... a spirit that delivered a white light. Preacher Jimmy and his gleeful flock had somehow been led to baptize their innards with their own brand of holy water.

Come to find out, Jimmy, who had been working as a trustee in the kitchen, had planned the caper for quite a while. He had, for some time now, been allowing a concoction of corn syrup, sugar, and God knows what else to ferment in the kitchen, somehow keeping the brew hid from prying eye and sensitive nose alike.

So when both time and conditions were "ripe" for revival, Jimmy stirred up the Elixir of Salvation (as he so fittingly ordained it) and somehow smuggled a hefty bit of it back up to his cell block after supper.

A prophet's foreordination was not needed to predict that Jimmy would be promptly relieved of his kitchen trustee duties ... and properly rewarded for his spirited church service with a new charge (which was later mercifully dropped).

Was it worth it?

No doubt, as Preacher Jimmy later told it, many a soul was saved from darkness ... for every sinner in seven block surely saw the light that night.

The Great White Ape of Steele Creek

(Dedicated to Steele Creek Nature Center and Steele Creek Park)

My little sister bought me the suit when I was in college. It was a lifelike gorilla suit, complete with mask, hands, and even feet. She spray-painted it white ... I suppose for camouflage since she bought it in winter.

I won't sojourn into the pranks I played with the Great White Ape suit at that particularly young and carefree time of my life, as many are a bit too ribald and rowdy for this book to hold.

Over time, it seems that both the suit and the legend of the Great White Ape converged together to take on a life all their own.

By the time I began teaching elementary school, I would intertwine lessons with stories of the legendary creature that just happened to inhabit the woods of our local Steele Creek Park.

One of the dearest friends I ever had, Glen Eads, and I were teaching at Highland View in a multi-age curriculum, where we taught all 4th, 5th and 6th graders in one room. In some sense, it was probably very much like the old-timey one-room schoolhouse.

We were planning to take an early spring field trip to hike at Steele Creek Park, so it was the perfect time to unwind a Great White Ape yarn.

The day before our trip, I "warned" the children about the legend. The story went something like this:

Back in the late Forties, a circus came through town and camped in the area that is now the Park.

I told of how one of the animal trainers kept an unusual gorilla encaged for children to see. This gorilla was an albino ape, lacking the darker skin and fur pigment of a regular great ape.

The Great White Ape, he was called by all.

In spite of its great size and strength, the Ape was shy and gentle. Somehow he had grown to love visits with children only.

Then one night, some cruel-minded boys snuck into the camp and came to the cage of the Great White Ape. There they prodded and poked him with long sharply-carved sticks until he bled.

The Ape didn't scream or even make a sound. He only sat there, deeply saddened, all the more so because it was children, not adults, who tortured him.

Finally, he silently bled to death … or so some say.

The next morning the Great White Ape's trainer found his blood-spattered cage empty. The huge steel bars were bent apart.

In front of the cage were large bloody footprints, which appeared to follow the tracks of a group of smaller footprints into the woods that are now Steele Creek Park.

A search party was quickly formed and followed the tracks.

Deep in the woods the smaller footprints suddenly disappeared. There appeared only the shoes, socks, and underwear of the boys (evidently these items weren't very tasty). Not another trace of the boys was ever found.

Now some folks will tell you, even today, the Great White Ape lives on in the woods of Steele Creek Park.

They say sometimes the Ape goes for days, or even weeks, without food *on purpose.*

(Now enters a big pause in my tale. Here the children usually ask the question, "Why?")

"Because ever since the night he was tortured, he will only eat … *children!*"

Of course, at this point, the children erupt with a series of cries and hollers loud enough to deafen most large primates.

So in a bit of a hushed tone, I remind them to be wary. "It's now early springtime of the year. Not many kids have ventured into those woods since last fall. So, as we hike through his territory tomorrow, keep in mind that the Great White Ape is going to be very, *very* … hungry!"

Again, utter pandemonium erupts, enough to make any real ape head for the hills.

So the legend lives on.

The next day, before the classes board the buses, Mr. Eads announces to the children that Mr. Talley has fallen ill and can't make the field trip.

On the way to the Park, some children begin to grow a bit more fearful of what might lurk deep in the woods along the trail.

As the children arrive at the Park and enter the forest, little do they know that yours truly is not ill, but alive and very well. I'm wearing the Great White Ape suit, hidden and lying in wait along the trail (all the while praying fervently that a big bad bear or curious coyote doesn't happen by).

Mr. Eads, with perfect timing, reiterates part of the legend, just as he leads the children into the deep woods. He warns them, "If you see the Ape, you should run straight down the hill toward the golf course."

(Probably the worst thing about fear is the "imagining" that something's out there. Whether that something is real or not makes little difference. To our physical senses, it can become as "real" as real can get, especially with children.)

Suddenly a white flash leaps out from behind a tree and charges toward the children. The Great White Ape has arrived. He begins throwing around fallen branches, roaring, and running toward the children.

I suppose anyone playing golf that day observed an unusual occurrence, as virtually all the children followed Mr. Eads' advice.

A child who lagged behind was grabbed by the beast. Named Bobbie Sue, she was captured and carried away toward the woods.

Unknown to the other children, the Ape immediately whispered to her, "Bobbie Sue, it's just me – Mr. Talley. You're okay. Just keep screaming like I'm real."

Several brave little souls charged straight on up the hill and into the woods to save Bobbie Sue. One child named Josh (who later aptly served in the armed forces) even tried to tackle me.

At which point the Great White Ape spun around, pulled off his mask, and grinned more like a big monkey than a gorilla.

The children cheered and all ran up the hill to hug the poor beloved creature.

Yes, the legend of the Great White Ape took on a life of its own.

From that day on, however, I refrained from initiating similar visits from the Ape, as my more prudent fellow teachers convinced me that I might get fired or sued.

Those thoughts honestly never entered my mind.

I'm proud to say, in nearly thirty years of sleigh-riding, cave-exploring, fossil excavating, and Great White Ape discovering, the worst injuries children have ever suffered under my care have been sprained ankles or bee stings. (Actually one kid felt the urge to run through a barbed wire fence once, just for the fun of it, but he was fine after a tetanus shot.)

One parent told me I've got a legion of guardian angels following me around, all working overtime. If true, I'm very grateful for their supervision and/or intervention, as the case may be, considering all the children who have gone on thrilling adventures with me over the years into the wild woods.

Full Moon Rises and Meteor Showers

(Dedicated to the Optimist Club of Bristol)

Few children get to take a hike these days.

Fewer still get to take a hike at night.

For a night hike, we'll often wait on a full moon, for a whole slew of reasons.

It's easier to see where you're walking, for one thing. After only a few minutes, the children become enchanted by how their eyes adapt to the lesser light of the night.

But what I like best about a full moon hike is that the children are wilder. At least, they think they are . . . which *makes* 'em wilder, I suppose.

I always enjoyed a wild, free-spirited child. It's easier to mold and steer such a child, than to do so with a completely fearful, timid kid.

I find it much more difficult to induce an inhibited child to free up and let their spirit soar.

Not so, a wild child.

For over ninety-nine percent of humanity's time on this planet, we've let our children play, almost exclusively, *outside*. Only in the last couple of generations have we lost this wonderful, natural, and utterly necessary outlet for our children.

It has certainly been my experience that kids in the wild listen much better, and learn much more, than they do in the classroom (although many are they in American public education today, without having observed firsthand the dichotomy of these experiences, who would probably assume that quite the opposite is true).

On full moon night hikes, even adults reawaken instincts long held dormant by modern society's obsession with our self-enforced technological walls.

Some of my fondest memories of night hikes are the sheer primal joys experienced by the larger and older members of our entourage. In a very real sense, a fully experienced night hike reacquaints us with the essence of what it means to be fully human on planet Earth.

And would a full moon hike be complete without a werewolf? I think not. I usually manage to find one who shows up at an opportune time, near the end of the hike. (There's always a big burly parent eager to play the part … with the help of a mask, well … usually.)

I've used night vision goggles on night hikes with kids, but I've found they're not necessary. They can also slow down the hike and invoke restlessness among the natives.

Besides, children are already astounded aplenty with what they can see and do at night with the unaided eye.

Sister Venus and Brother Mars are nearly always parading about up high, yearning to introduce themselves to a new generation of children. Oh, and how starry-eyed the children become, once they're introduced to the free nightly buffet of wonders offered beyond the scope of our home planet.

Of course telescopes are welcomed, as we scour the heavens for more distant planets and view the face of the Man on the Moon closer up.

At night in the wild woods our primordial instincts are stirred and we feel deep down to the bone what our ancestors must have felt.

Every emotion is heightened.

Every fear felt full.

Every joy enjoyed rapturously.

One of the most beautiful, and most memorable, sites a child will likely ever see is a full moon rising over the horizon through the woods. Yet in today's world of electronic gadgetry gods, so few children now know this innate and unspeakable joy.

Speaking of gods, we also do some constellation gazing, akin to our forefathers. In the winter months, the children always seem especially enraptured by Orion the Hunter (as have countless other waifs, no doubt, stretched back across countless generations to humanity's cradle).

I'm not certain why, but I've found that when a child learns to love the stars, they seem to forever find it more difficult to intentionally inflict harm upon a fellow earthly being.

One wonderful November night (when we *didn't* want a full moon) I lay flat on my back with nearly one hundred little urchins and their families. We had assembled to watch the Leonid meteor shower put on her annual show. Climbing high up a meadow-draped hill on a dark, clear, moonless night – we relished a night perfect for wishing on "falling stars".

I fancy any child who was there can tell you about it to this day.

It's not likely those same children can recall the words to their third spelling test of that year.

Or tell you where they were the very moment they learned to find the area of a rectangle.

And I'd be willing to bet all the wishes I've ever made that they can't recall dropping their jaw in awe the day they learned the state capital of Idaho.

Oh, the night time sky, it does show us much about who we were, who we are, and where we're going … when we slow down enough to look up.

The Night Time Sky

(Dedicated to Abuse Alternatives locally, and all agencies everywhere who serve and protect victims of domestic abuse)

Speaking of the night time sky, I found that the ancient astrologers were right about something ... something which I had previously considered complete and utter superstition - that the stars *can* indeed be used to reveal our futures.

How they were right, however, proved to be in a far grander context than even their wide-open minds had perhaps ever imagined.

It began with a simple homework assignment: I told my students to watch the night time sky.

I was doing my student teaching at the old Douglass Elementary School in Bristol, Virginia.

Back in the day of racial segregation, Douglass had been a school for African-American students only. Even during my stint as a student teacher, the school still served the vast majority of the city's black students.

It was one of those bright, clear October blue-sky days. I gave my fourth graders a simple assignment. They were to go out after dark and observe the night time sky for five minutes. Then they were to come back in and write a paragraph about what they experienced.

. . .

(Since my own childhood, I have always tried to take at least a brief moment each evening to cast my eyes toward the night time sky. Weather permitting, I rarely miss a night. This nightly communion with the creation, gaping up wide-eyed at the grandeur of the heavens, seems to bring me a sense of silent joy. Without wishing or pleading for a single thing, I often come away filled with a deep peace that things down here are never quite as bad as they may seem, or maybe not even bad at all . . . and I wanted the children to have at least a little taste of the same.)

. . .

So the next morning after giving the assignment to watch the night time sky, I asked my student Timmy to go first.

Timmy mumbled and grumbled and made excuses (which was his way). As he stomped to the front of the class, Timmy read the following:

"I don't know why we had to do this stupid assignment. I call it stupid because it was cold out and my mother kept yelling at me to come in and clean my room the whole time. I didn't see anything anyway. The moon wasn't even full. You could hardly see any stars because some clouds came wanderin' in. It wasn't clear like you said it would be. It was just a dark and cloudy night."

I can't say we were surprised at Timmy's words, but I can say we were shocked.

Virtually every other student who followed Timmy had nothing but positive remarks when relating their experiences with the night time sky.

Especially Natalie.

Natalie (who, as a preferred means of locomotion, seemed to "bound" her way through life) bounded right up the aisle to the front of the class and read the following:

"The first thing I noticed was the moon. It wasn't full, but if I held my head sideways it smiled down at me every time. The moon tried to shine, even though it was dark and cloudy. It was also colder than I thought it would be, but I didn't mind. I was having too much fun. The few stars that I found twinkled their happiness down. Then the dark fluffy clouds passed right by in front of the smiling moon. I called them black sheep, like me. I hope we do this again."

I can't say we were surprised by Natalie's words either, though I can say that most of us sat with a muted sense of reverence and awe as she read them.

Had they looked closely, the class may have even noticed that I shed a quiet tear or two.

My tears were not begotten of joy. They were born of a profound sadness that suddenly seemed to capture my senses.

I suppose that's not an uncommon reaction, when one realizes one is in the presence of an angelic spirit who appears doomed by everything life can throw at her . . . but doesn't even know it.

Natalie's race had nothing to do with her handicap. But ignorance and poverty did.

Her only chance was getting a good education, the one Great Equalizer in our nation. But Natalie stood little chance at that.

I wanted to help her somehow, but I knew she and her mother would likely be up and gone at a moment's notice, in the middle of some night soon.

Despite the astronomical odds against her in this life, Natalie had a way of finding good in everything that came her way.

When I first met her, Natalie had lived for several days in an abandoned van with her mother and little brother. They were scared and on the run, victims of domestic abuse.

Natalie often wore the same clothes to school two or three times a week.

By the way, Timmy wore nice clothes to school. He lived in a three bedroom house. Both his parents were gainfully employed.

When every child had finished reading about their own experience, I asked the class, "Did everyone look up at the same night time sky?"

Most children didn't yet understand. Remembering Timmy's description, most gave an affirmative "No!"

A few gave a soft, but clear, "Yes!" They understood that everyone looked at the same sky, but saw it in different ways.

Yes, Timmy and Natalie gazed up at the same night time sky.

Yet they stood worlds apart in what they saw. Staggered by the compelling influence of both attitudes, as the years passed on, I thought often of how their lives might turn out.

. . .

I keep up with every child I ever taught, as best I can. Natalie and Timmy were no exceptions.

But Natalie got lost in the fog of life, and I didn't have any idea under the heavens where she might be. I was always hoping that something about her would pop up again through the mist.

It didn't.

With Timmy, it did.

Timmy, it seems, continued to mumble and grumble and stomp his way through life. He dropped out of high school and got acquainted with a street gang in Johnson City.

I'll never forget the moment I found out Timmy's end.

I had just ordered my meal at a restaurant in Bristol with my son and two other former students. Suddenly a young man named Dean, whom I'd taught at the same time as Timmy and Natalie, came over to greet me. Dean was working in the kitchen as a cook. He happened to see me and came out to share some old times.

I had to ask about Timmy.

Dean replied, "Oh, man, you haven't heard? Timmy's funeral was just last week. He got shot in the back of the head outside a night club in Johnson City."

That evening was one of the few times in my life I left a plate full of food untouched.

As for Natalie, well, she still remained lost in the fog.

I remembered vividly that she had wanted to become a nurse. But I knew her grades were weak and her poverty strong. A realist would say she had two chances to make her dreams come true – slim and none.

Natalie hadn't even been in my class but a few weeks, when Mom up and moved the family in the middle of one night, ever on the run from abuse.

Indeed, the deck of life was stacked ponderously against Natalie in almost every conceivable way imaginable.

I never tell kids that they can be whatever they want to be, because that's about as big and cruel a lie as I could ever tell them.

We all have our limitations. I couldn't be an NFL lineman. Nor could I be a concert pianist . . . or even the world's greatest underwater basket weaver. It wouldn't matter how hard I tried.

There are many ways to bring good to this world. So I used what I had.

Natalie's one great redeeming strength (to counter the whole world being stacked against her) was the unquenchable, uplifting hope she brought to every single soul who crossed her path.

So I told her, again and again during our brief time together, that she would wind up helping people as a way of life. I absolutely guaranteed it and promised her it would happen.

I even asked her to try to let me know someday when it came true, because I was truly convinced that it would . . . I just didn't know how.

. . .

More than four thousand night time skies had traversed the heavens since I had last taught Natalie. A child's lifetime of crescent moons had smiled sideways from above since I had last heard her voice.

One evening, as I was outside in the back yard surveying the celestial canopy, my cell phone rang.

"Mr. Talley, this is Natalie Jones. Do you remember me?"

I sputtered out a "Yes." I couldn't compose myself enough to tell her that her sprightly spirit had never faded from my memory all these years.

She continued on, her voice almost trembling with elation. "I wanted to let you know that I'm getting to help people. I'm going to be a nurse! I just graduated from UT and . . ."

This time, the drops that traced my cheeks were not born of sadness.

They were conceived of joy, a cherished gift from an angelic spirit who saw nothing but the light of good . . . no matter how dark or cloudy raged the night.

Jesus Was a Hillbilly

(Dedicated to those souls in our region who proudly speak the King's English with an Appalachian drawl and dialect)

We all know it's not unusual for some folks from around our nation, and even the world, to gaze a bit down their noses toward the people of our Southern Appalachian Highlands.

I find the main reason for this show of disrespect can largely be traced to one primary trait of our region's people – the colorful dialect /accent by which we speak the English language. I've certainly experienced this sense of contempt myself, as has the native reader, no doubt, when travelling away from our elevated homeland.

Some from beyond (and even within) our region make the mistake of referring to the way we speak as "country".

We speak "hillbilly", sir and madam, as we live in a mountainous land. "Country", my dear linguists, is spoken further down South, the abode of flatlanders.

Whenever I venture to other terrain on the map, my mountain accent/dialect guides everyone within earshot toward my turf of birth. When I speak, all doubt of my ancestral origin is removed.

The assumption that an entire people's general intelligence might be deduced from their particular elocution of the native language, although I find it disturbing, surprises me not.

What perplexes me far more is the fact that I've found too many of our own native folk who are admittedly ashamed of their distinctly Appalachian articulation. Yes, a surprising number of our homegrown mountain clan would, if they could, trade in their drawling tongue.

To those who would do so, I cry, "Blasphemy!" in my most assuredly authentic hillbilly diction.

Several years ago now, I wrote the following personal letter to Ms. Andrea Mitchell, NBC news correspondent (and a lady whom I happen to actually admire and like) following an internationally televised comment in which she insulted and defamed the honorable people of our Appalachian region. Somehow I never mailed the letter, but I found it did me unspeakable good to write it.

Here is the letter, in its proud colloquial entirety:

By the way, Ms. Mitchell, Jesus was a hillbilly too.

Yep, it's the Gospel Truth. Jesus was a bona fide hillbilly, a heap of a whole lot like us present-day Appalachian Mountain folk. And if'n you're already a-countin' yourself among the unbelievers, be prepared to repent and be born again.

Yep, Ms. Mitchell, you can take the boy out of the hills, but you simply can't take the hills out of the boy. If we could, we might ask Jesus' right hand disciple, Simon Peter.

Ms. Mitchell (I know you know this already), the followin' scene took place on the night of Jesus' crucifixion:

The Bible tells how a bunch of them big city Jerusalem tattletales figured out Simon Peter to be a bona fide high country Galilean. You see, Ms. Mitchell, it was all by them listenin' to his peculiar accent and dialect while he, as Peter was highly prone to do, went on blabberin' a bit too much. (Bein' human, you and I both know about how that type of thing can happen.)

Ms. Mitchell, I think you'll agree that we all speak from our childhood with every word we utter.

Anyone growin' up with a New York City accent/dialect will carry that cross to their grave.

Likewise, any child of these here Appalachian Mountains will do the same.

Now, with Jerusalem bein' the "New York City" of ancient Israel, and Galilee representin' America's hill country "Appalachia", it don't take no great leap of faith to see why Jesus' disciples could be so rightly geographically placed by their manner of speech alone.

Ms. Mitchell, I even looked it up on one of them newfangled geography sites online. That little ole village of Nazareth, where Jesus spent almost His entire life, why it was set above sea level just about presactly the same height as my hometown of Bristol!

And you know that fellow Nathaniel in John's book of the Good Book? Why, he asked a question a whole lot like you might have asked back then.

The Good Book records Nathaniel as askin', "Can anything good come out of Nazareth?"

You see, even way back then, Nathaniel and them city boys perceived us folks from the hills as havin' a type of crude culture, with a quaint sort of language.

Well, I'm right proud to say that they was right about the latter perception . . . but they was downright wrong about the former. There plum ain't no friendlier place on a map than in these here hills (as long as you don't commence to makin' fun of us).

I reckon it to be a fact, Ms. Mitchell - since Jesus was raised in a place a lot like where I'm from, it goes to show you that in these here hills, we know how to bring up good people.

Now, Ms. Mitchell, there are some good folk out there (and you might number among 'em) who plain old don't understand my hillbilly way of understandin' Jesus. I just tell 'em it's downright scriptural.

No sacrilege is intended here at all. Quite the opposite is true.

Ms. Mitchell, as you know, it's widely agreed that Jesus came for the benefit of all. But it seems that Jesus came particularly to the misrepresented, the misunderstood, the poor, and the persecuted.

Now, Ms. Mitchell, you'd have to think mighty hard to come up with a class of folk more misrepresented, misunderstood, poorer, or more persecuted than the common hillbilly (this one might really ring a bell somewhere for you).

And you can bet your big city loaves and fishes that the greatest Hillbilly of 'em all moved his tongue in tune to a big ole mountain drawl.

Yep, Ms. Mitchell, the life that changed all others was lived largely in the Galilean hill country, among the common, salt-of-the-earth folk of Jesus' incomparable parables. It would do us all, hillbillies and big city folk alike, more than two mites of good to mutually acknowledge that The Greatest Life Ever Lived spoke with a twang looked down upon by much of the world of his day - and ours.

Yep. It's true. Jesus was a hillbilly. And it's just plain old logic, Ms. Mitchell, not an act of blind faith, that guides us toward the overwhelmin' historical evidence.

But wait . . . my hillbilly intuition tells me that somebody out there's gonna swear on a stack of Bibles that it's already been plum downright inerrantly revealed that God the Father Almighty truly and forever speaks only in perfectly monotone King James English.

And if'n you don't believe me, just ask somebody who claims to know the whole Truth (particularly if it's pertainin' to religion). Because believe me, Ms. Mitchell, in these here hills, just the same as in your big city . . . there ain't no shortage of folks who know everything.

By the way, Ms. Mitchell, we really do forgive you for insultin' us so unfavorably. I'm sure neither you nor Nathaniel meant to talk about us quite as badly as it came out.

But look at it this way, at least your insult wasn't written down in a book that's been read by about a gazillion people for thousands of years now. Poor Nathaniel, he got it way worse than you.

But we forgive him too. You see, we've been taught . . . it's the Hillbilly thing to do.

Pregnant Children, Pointless Paperwork, and Dead Puppies

(Dedicated to every public and private school teacher on both sides of our beloved town, throughout our region, throughout the world)

The words hurt. "You teachers are lucky. You really don't have to work that much."

A friend from my childhood had called me. We hadn't shared words in nigh four decades, which only made the conversation all the more cherished. A friend from childhood is a friend forever.

We were alternately laughing and talking along happily when he suddenly said something that stung me. "You teachers are lucky. You really don't have to work that much."

I assumed he was alluding to a belief that perhaps I didn't work as hard as he did in his own very honorable vocation.

I didn't want to argue with an old friend, especially after not talking with him in so many years, so I changed the subject back to our childhood days.

But later on that night, as I lay wide awake, my thoughts tumbled again toward my old friend.

So the next morning I decided to keep a diary of what I did during the day:

I awake at 4:45, although my alarm is set for 6:00. I toss and turn for fifteen more minutes, thinking of Donnie. I fussed at him yesterday, something a good teacher tries hard not to do. I suppose that's why he listened . . . because I rarely fuss. At least that's what I tell myself, as I rise to type replies to emails sent to me from the night before.

Usually at least a handful (of my now nearly two

thousand) ex-students email me, on the average, each night.

But one email from this previous night had stayed up with me, tormenting my sleep, far more so than my old friend's remarks.

A former student, now an 18-year-old senior in high school, a straight-A student for years, is pregnant . . . and she is asking my advice.

What do I say?

I tell myself that a good teacher doesn't shrug off life's crises, but teaches students how to face them.

All throughout the day, Eva's email will haunt me. At little intervals, sometimes two minutes, others lasting only the flash of a second, my mind will revisit her request, ever searching for a wise reply.

I arrive early to school so I can talk to Willie, who I appointed as a safety patrol to hold open the front door for the other kids as they enter the school. He lives a troubled life, and I just want to make sure I tell him I appreciate him, just for who he is.

Our students are not separated from us when we leave school. We carry them on with us where ever we go.

During the course of a day, I play psychologist, nurse, coach, and social worker. I wear many hats.

And I must be quickly adaptable to each child and their unique situation. None are ever exactly the same. Not ever.

And I must make perhaps a thousand snap decisions during the course of a normal day, each of which will affect the lives of children forever.

That's a long time.

I laugh a lot during the day, providing a general atmosphere of "play" with the children a large percentage of the time, which is how tons of research (and even more common sense) tell us that children learn best.

I find out at lunch why one of my students is absent today. His mother had to enter the hospital. I make plans to visit after school . . . when I feel my best teaching begins.

When the school door slams shut behind me, I hit the open woods and trails of Sugar Hollow Park for an hour, scouting and note-taking for a butterfly/wildflower hike we are soon to take one Saturday, when my students will meet me of their own free will (which I've found that children and their families actually love to do, given the chance).

Just after the hospital visit to the student's sick mother, I hop over to a Little League baseball game and wolf down a hot dog . . . or two. I've found that families rarely forget when a teacher shows up to watch their children perform in an after-school event.

My own family has always been a constant part of my after-school teaching life.

For years my wife and family availed Christmas gatherings for my students and their families in our home and, come warmer weather, we entertained them with food aplenty at overnight campouts in our back yard.

Indeed, my teenage son spent part of this same evening helping me plan the upcoming Saturday hike, as he has done for literally countless hikes and events over the years of his growing up. He will tell you to this day his life has only been enriched by such a way of living and giving.

Before dusk, I make a drive-by visit to the family of a child I taught long ago. We teachers do this type of thing, not because we think we can make a big difference in their lives, but because we think we can make a little one.

A childlike voice speaks to me from within. It tells me, in words both silent and strong, that as time marches us all inescapably onward toward the grave, those little differences will eventually become big.

The fact that we seldom live to see the full results of our efforts serves to strengthen our faith . . . and our humility.

I arrive home after dark, but my day is not over. I must now create exciting lesson plans to inspire over one hundred children tomorrow.

At my side, I have a pile of mundane (but deemed

governmentally necessary) paperwork staring me in the face. This particular paperwork is pointless to the nth degree, maybe a factor of ten past meaningless. No one can tell me how it has been proven to help children. They can only tell me "it has to be done".

To a creative, risk-taking, right-brained thinker who's never voluntarily initiated an orderly, organized, left-brained thought in his life, there's almost nothing worse on this Earth than having to do completely pointless paperwork.

But . . . to keep my job, I do it anyway, whether or not I find any real meaning in it.

I don't ever want a child to find any of my classroom lessons meaningless . . . unconventional, off-the-wall, or crazy maybe . . . but never meaningless.

While my attention-deficit-disordered mind muffles through the mind-numbing paperwork, it alternately brainstorms lesson plans for tomorrow. The faint, but very appealing, thought of a "simple machine classroom scavenger hunt" gradually settles itself somewhere into the back of my brain.

All the while I feel my mind pulsating back and forth, contemplating my promised reply to the pregnant ex-student, which I promised to send to her this night.

Suddenly a few words come to me and I grow at peace with them. I type my reply.

Then my phone rings.

It's a little girl, one of my current students. I glance at the clock and wonder why she's up so late. She's sobbing softly, but I can still make out her words.

She tells me that her puppy just got killed by a car in front of her house. She had asked her parents if she could call me.

"I knew you'd want to know about it," she grieves. "Will you help me bury him tomorrow, sometime after school?"

I decide that my childhood friend was right. Teachers are lucky . . . and we really don't have to work that much.

In fact, for the most part, I would hesitate to refer to what I do as work. Nor would I choose to call it a job or a grind.

I would prefer to call it a privilege . . . or a calling . . . or both.

A Misidentification of Gemstones

(Dedicated to all those who provide counseling
services for children)

Men are from Mars and women from Venus. Or so the
old saying goes.

I originally believed there was not *that* much of a
difference between the thinking of boys and girls, at
least not as early as fifth grade.

One day, a particular boy and girl helped me see both
Mars and Venus more clearly than ever before.

By the way, regarding the genuinely scientific topic of
"the birds and the bees", I would readily acknowledge
from my experience that girls do mature faster than boys,
both physically and emotionally.

But boys . . . oh, boy . . . they do seem to fly and buzz
sooner.

. . .

Roger came bellowing into my classroom, fresh from a
battle-ball game the kids had played in gym. (Roger
bellowed his way through life, and I fancy, still does, where
ever his bellicose soul may now reside.)

Grabbing himself between his legs, Roger howled in
mock pain, "I lost my family jewels in the gym!"

Of course, being in a public school, and with young
females around, I reacted to this epithet quite differently
than I might have, say, on a camping trip with all boys.

I calmed Roger's bellow down to a guffaw . . . then to
a mutter, before allowing him to say another word related
to gemstones.

Most girls giggled (whether they knew what they were
giggling at or not).

Most boys snickered (for quite a different reason –the words "mutual empathy" might well suffice).

I firmly told Roger that his choice of words was not appropriate for school.

To which he bellowed out, "Do you want me to call 'em by their real name?"

More giggles and snickers arose, but just as quickly died away due to my withering gaze (which social convention dictated I must now throw toward all).

Then Sally (who, it must be noted, lived with no brothers, one little sister, and her mother) raised her hand and called out, "But, Mr. Talley, Roger means he lost something valuable, like rubies or emeralds."

There was nothing but utter and complete silence for a moment. I thought to myself, this little girl (who was one of my kindest students), as usual, is way ahead of the game. She's getting Roger out of trouble, lightening up the tone of the class, and giving us all a chance to escape from the whole predicament with honor - all in one fell swoop.

"That's very clever, Sally. I agree that's exactly what Roger meant . . . and nothing else. So let's get on with class, okay?"

We continued with class (in spite of an occasional, barely audible, chortle from a boy or two), when Sally again raised her hand.

She looked at me incredulously and asked, "Mr. Talley, don't you think someone should go check the gym?"

"For what?" I asked.

Sally's innocent eyes stared back at me, more puzzled than ever. In fact she was almost angry (an emotion rarely seen on her sweet face). Her voice quavered with sincere indignation as she spoke, "Mr. Talley, you shouldn't treat boys any differently than you would girls. If I'd lost *my* jewels in the gym, you'd let me go back and look, now, wouldn't you?"

I held out the faintest hope that she was continuing to display an advanced sense of humor.

All such hopes vanished when the poor child quickly looked toward Roger and added, "I've got a book about gemstones at home. I can identify them all. Just tell me what your jewels look like, Roger, and if Mr. Talley will let me, I'll go look for them myself."

The boys roared with laughter so loud they shook the rafters. And … whether social convention merited it or not … so did I.

Lest ye think me nothing but a cruel knave, I must make mention of my visit to kind Sally's home after school that day, whereupon I turned redder than a ruby, sputtering out an explanation to Mom about her daughter's recent classroom gaffe.

I've got a feeling that Sally got the birds and the bees talk from her mother that very evening. Certainly, I never heard her misidentify gemstones in such a way again.

Christmas Caroling and Bell Ringing

(Dedicated to Bristol's Salvation Army . . . and all those special people who care for the elderly in our region)

(a take-home flyer sent to all students near Christmas-time)

Dear Parents (of my one-hundred and twenty-two wonderful little volunteers),

For Christmas Caroling, please meet me at the Van Pelt Elementary School parking lot no later than 6 p.m. Monday, Tuesday, or Wednesday evening ... which ever evening you choose to join us!

Remember, "car pooling" is appreciated. If dropping off your child, please come back by 9 to pick them up (or else they'll have to spend the night with Santa).

Remember, we'll first go to Bristol Nursing Home. Nowhere else on earth are children appreciated more. Some of the ladies will even be found holding dolls, in lieu of their long-gone children.

Then on we'll go to the Bristol Jail to carol the lady inmates there. (Not to worry – your wee tykes will be perfectly safe.) These ladies miss their children and will cherish hearing yours sing to them.

Also, below is the sign-up list for our upcoming Salvation Army bell-ringing at Wal-Mart (main entrance). The Salvation Army is much underserved this year, but the needy are still needy. This opportunity is yet another worthy (and fun!) way to teach our children to serve their community . . . . and they can take turns ringing that bell!

It will most certainly be fine to drop off your child and return to pick them up (parents are welcome to stay, if you wish).

They'll be safe and secure with me at all times. (By the way, anyone who brings us hot chocolate will not make us angry.) And certainly more than one child can come at the same time. I say the more the merrier!

Mr. T.

423-797-_ _ _ _ (Please tear off the form at the line below and return to me – thank you!)

My child, _____, will come help Mr. T. ring a bell for those in need this special time of year:

Please check your time(s) and return to Mr. T.

Wed. 4:00-5:00 ___ 5:00-6:00 ___ 6:00-7:00 ___ 7:00-8:00__

Fri. 4:00-5:00 ___ 5:00-6:00 ___ 6:00-7:00 ___ 7:00-8:00__

The previous flyer attests to tidings of great joy.

I know not of an equal anywhere on the calendar. What fonder time of year is there than the festive winter holidays?

As one can see from the flyer, we invite all children to participate in the holiday celebration by visiting/serving the most needy of our community.

Our visits to the Bristol Nursing Home are a sure cure for dry eyes.

Once, on elderly female resident began singing right along with the children from her wheelchair. I was told this lady had hardly spoken a word in years.

As we all moved on down the hall, I glanced back. I couldn't help but notice how a mask of emotionless melancholy slowly returned to haunt her face.

At least for a moment the children had given her soul a wisp of joy, however brief.

Ladies, once vibrant and quick-witted, now know little more than to cuddle baby dolls.

Ah, but even senility-ravaged minds perk up at the sound of children's voices! More magical than any medicine, the mere sight and sound of young children can revive emotions long ago thought dead in the old.

To the Bristol Jail we go next, where the female inmates tip-toe up as high as they can to peer through the bars. If they stretch, they can see us singing in the grassy courtyard below. Often, the ladies join in caroling with us.

We have made Christmas cards for each of these ladies, which I delivered earlier. They contain a lot of children's art and sweet words, but I make sure every card says, "Take care of your children." Some may think these words a bit harsh, but I know of nothing kinder we could say. Nearly all of these ladies have children, some of whom I've taught in my classroom.

And parents only know lasting happiness in this world when they are good parents. Otherwise, they will never know peace on Earth within their hearts . . .

The ladies continue yelling out "Merry Christmas!" and "Thank you, little kids!" long after we've turned to go.

Perhaps no one we carol appreciates it more than the lady who resides at our next destination.

My mother (who was still living at the time of this flyer) welcomes us, each and all, with homemade cookies. Not only that, but she has painstakingly made a homemade candy-cane reindeer for each child. She does this every Christmas for the children I teach, though her hands and eyes move a bit slower with each passing year.

Before leaving my mother, every child both gives and receives one of life's longest remembered gifts . . . a genuine hug.

Everyone practically skips back to the parking lot. The unmitigated joy of giving appears to illicit such a response from children.

(I think to myself how these children, given the opportunity, all appear so innately *eager* to give and to share. Is it somehow "instinctive" in us to give and to share, as a way to survive? My mind wanders to a quote from the late great astronomer, Carl Sagan, "The vastness of the universe boggles the human mind. This vastness is only made bearable through one thing - love.")

Finally, to somewhere that's found most easily in this town - the home of gracious parents - for hot chocolate.

All in all, we carol and visit for three nights, making sure every child has transportation and the opportunity to go at least once.

Ringing bells and singing carols with your friends as a way to better the lives of others less fortunate . . . surely

few more festive ways exist to make merry the
heart of childhood.

Standing outside of Wal-Mart in a snowstorm, the
children and I receive several hundred dollars worth of
change for the Salvation Army each night. It appears to be
difficult for even the most hardened soul to pass by such a
frolicsome site without dropping down at least a dime.

It's cold outside, but the children stay warm by singing
and laughing. No need for a stove or a heater out here.
There's probably no greater warmth in Bristol than on these
cold, snowy nights when children exhibit their care for the
needy of our good town and region.

Our Greatest Gift

(Dedicated to every outdoor children's camp … and to those wise caregivers and parents who let kids play outside)

If one wanted to predict humanity's future, one might do well by watching children "play" at one of our local Survival Camps.

No, not *that* kind of Survival Camp! I promise I don't drop the little urchins off in the middle of the wild on the coldest night of winter with only their underwear and a pocket knife (though, if I ever did, quite a few would surprise us all, I have no doubt).

I intentionally set up Survival Camp as a microcosm of life.

The only thing I do *for* the children is at the beginning. I intentionally group them into small "tribes" of my own choosing.

Most of course would rather group with their "friends". I'm very open and honest with them as to why I group them with other children who, as I tell them, "will soon become" their friends. I tell them that by the end of the day they'll be surprised by what all they accomplish and that they just need to trust me.

I go over the rules and activities, which can vary quite a bit, depending on the season of the year and type of terrain on which we'll traverse. But, in general, Survival Camp activities will go something like the following:

Your tribe will find a place to sleep in the woods for the night. The campsite must be safe and not within fifty yards of another tribe (they often step off the distance, or estimate with a homemade yard "stick"). The site must also be within one hundred yards of a source of running water.

You will make a clay pottery drinking cup for each member of your tribe. (This one sounds tough, but I make sure the clay is not hard to find, and I provide crude oral instructions on mixing in some dry grass and a bit of water. It's absolutely stunning how the children will stick with this, experimenting with various ingredients and textures over and over, until they have something that remarkably resembles pottery.)

You will each climb a designated cliff (no, not *that* big of a cliff!), helping each other to the top. (I try to choose at least one "demonstrably clumsy" soul for each tribe. That way, this activity can only be completed if teamwork is devised and applied throughout.}

You will gather various berries, nuts, or edible plants (I show a sample of what might be in the area to each group at the onset). A point is given for each type gathered. All these points are nullified if a group gathers a toxic berry or plant. (This insures safety and stresses consensus among the group. Besides, they're not allowed to eat anything until I say so.)

You will create a tribal song (and accompanying music, if desired). Sticks and stones can do wonders here for background percussion. I've seen wild vines fashioned into stringed instruments and some fabulous woodwinds hollowed out from sticks.

Your tribe will build a stone campfire circle, replete with tinder and wood, stacked properly for sustained burning on the first strike of a match. (We rarely actually light the campfires, and certainly not in a city park, but I can tell pretty well whether their assemblage will burn at first strike or not.)

You will make at least one fair trade (of either materials or knowledge) with each tribe. You will gain two points for each fair trade made (the trade must benefit both tribes, not just one).

You are encouraged to discuss things among your tribe. (Of course, there are inevitable disagreements, but how they *solve* these disagreements can lead to as many as ten points.)

You will choose a tribal name for your group and for each individual. Every member must agree that this name "fits" for some good reason. Names cannot be derogatory.

All decisions are to be made by group consensus, *not* majority vote.

Tribes often face exasperation and want to do a "majority vote", when all can't decide what they think is best. Sometimes I'll hear something like, "But that's the democratic way, to vote on it."

Group "consensus" is something new for many (and certainly would be for many adults). It's surprising what can be accomplished when everyone truly feels their opinion is valued. When solving problems, why don't we aim more often for "thoughtful consensus" in place of "majority rule" when working as adults? It sure works with kids! (I so very much wish every member of Congress could watch them in action.)

Each tribe will try to find items on a Scavenger Hunt list. (They don't keep the items, only locate them.) Things like: a feather, a water-weathered rock, a snail, a bird in flight, cumulus clouds, the oldest living thing in the forest, the tallest tree in our area, fungi, humus soil, and so on.

Once the inter-tribal camaraderie/information sharing begins, it's not unusual for the kids to find all of one hundred items on a list, no matter how difficult I may try to make it.

Fighting over "territory" is not allowed. We all share the land. Ten points is added if you resolve all disputes over territory. (I found out early on that even little primates are extremely territorial. No wonder we humans grow up to kill one another over borders!)

Kids, if unfettered by adults, will showcase our species' greatest asset at Survival Camps - *they will naturally teach each other.*

"Lord of The Flies" type selfishness might happen if the children were left without an acting facilitator. But as long as there's someone there to "guide and teach" (like yours truly) I've seen small groups of children exhibit cooperative altruism that would be the envy of all nations.

I'm always around to guide and teach the tykes, but only when absolutely needed. "Discovery" learning is kept at an optimum.

If finished before the others, a tribe will learn what the needs of the other tribes are and try to teach them how to meet their needs.

"Giving away something for nothing" is not allowed. Fair trades and "teaching how" are allowed and encouraged.

The mutual benefit to every tribe that comes from no tribe being left "poor" is encouraged to be discovered, as well.

Finally, we restore everything as close as possible to the way we found it.

Please don't think these Camps are all "boy" stuff. Quite the contrary, I've found that if I group tribes by gender, girls often tend to score higher on these Survival Camps.

Perhaps it's because girls tend to be less aggressive, less confrontational, and less competitive among themselves as do boys. I'm not sure.

I'm also not sure that if women were to someday head every nation, that the nations of the world would be so quick to go to war as a way to settle conflicts as they do now. And, yes, boys (and men) are quite capable of placing mutual cooperation over selfish competition, too. But . . . it's a bit rarer in my gender, we of the more aggressive, competitive hormones (which do indeed have their time and place).

When all is said and done, I fancy it would be difficult for one to observe our Survivor Camps without an empowered sense of hope for humanity's future.

Mother Nature really does know best.

And to see Mother *at* her best, in a way that we rarely even glimpse in our modern culture, just let children go play in the wild woods.

I feel like Margaret Mead (the great anthropologist who studied Stone Age tribes in New Guinea for decades) when

I watch the various behaviors exhibited by children at play in the wild woods.

We know that many children of other animals "play at" the various social survival skills which they'll someday need as adults. So why don't we do more of this for our own children ... let them "play to learn"?

Indeed, Survival Camps have shown me firsthand:

Children learn more when engaged by a healthy "mix" of individual competition *and* group collaboration - which might help explain some of our culture's seemingly incurable infatuation with sports!

Children learn best when their natural sense of "play" is not constrained, but encouraged.

Children are all potentially magnificent teachers. It is perhaps our species' greatest gift, whether we live in Appalachia or Anatolia; to teach, to pass along a learned skill or knowledge to one another. I marvel at how even the shyest child grows *immediately eager to teach another* when a new skill is learned or a discovery made.

Bristol Little League

(Dedicated to all those who serve youth sports – may you forever remember that they long remember you)

Baseball in Bristol is big. Even with the rise of soccer (yes, it's also a great sport), baseball is still as American as apple pie and fly fishing.

I loved my many years associated with coaching a baseball team in Bristol Little League.

Some of my fondest teaching moments were spent coaching. A good coach is a good teacher, no doubt . . . and vice versa.

However, I'd have to say that some of my worst moments involved coaching also . . . and they were almost always my fault.

I once coached a kid named Ralphie.

Ralphie was so fast he could pass some kids on our team running backwards.

Which gave me an idea . . .

Before one game I told Ralphie that, just for the fun of it (the reason for many things I did as a coach), he ought to run around the bases by starting toward third base, instead of going toward first base. I told him to run all the bases at full speed in reverse order, no matter where the other kids were throwing the ball.

I added that he should never slow down for a second, no matter what happened, until he slid into home plate.

I knew Ralphie would be called out, even if he made it home safely, but it would be a ton of fun to watch.

Of course, Ralphie's being safe or out wasn't the point. I just wanted the kids to have some memorable fun . . . and enjoy a little mischief with the umpire that day (who was

notoriously straight-laced about everything from
baseball rules to how he tied his shoes).

Ralphie, our leadoff hitter, walked up to home plate and
hit the first pitch thrown to him.

The shortstop who fielded Ralphie's routine ground ball
got so confused that he hesitated a bit before he threw the
ball toward *third* base (because that's where Ralphie was
headed) instead of first base.

Well, by the time the now-bewildered third-
baseman could think where to throw the ball, Ralphie's
speed had allowed him to pass third.

Ralphie now headed for second base.

The befuddled third baseman threw the ball to second,
but the ball arrived again too late to nab Ralphie.

The baffled second baseman threw the ball toward first
(as Ralphie rampaged on), but . . . well, you can guess . . .
Ralphie had already turned first base and was headed for
home plate. He slid across home plate with blazing speed
just ahead of the first baseman's throw.

The home plate umpire was so flabbergasted that he
initially called Ralphie safe. Then he sputtered around a
bit, realizing that couldn't possibly be right, and called
him out.

The coach for the other team (a great sport, as I found
most youth coaches to be in our good town) finally caught
his breath enough to shout out, "I don't care if he's safe or
out, ump! That was worth my team giving up a run just to
watch. I've never seen anything like it."

Neither had anyone else there that day . . . and likely
never will again.

After the game, when the teams stood at home plate and
shook hands with each other (as we always did to show
sportsmanship), Ralphie and a couple of kids took off
running toward third base. Suddenly every kid on my team
took off running ... the wrong way around the bases.
I grabbed the ump by the arm and pulled him along with me,
as we chugged toward third base, following the gleeful

throng. It was such a thrill that even an iron-clad "letter of the law" soul couldn't possibly resist. By the time the ump and I crossed home plate, I'll wager he was having at least as much fun as any kid there that day . . . whether it was in the rule book or not.

Another time I sent a kid up to bat wearing a White Ape mask.

I also had our pitcher throw a tennis ball toward home plate during a game.

We had fun, that's for sure. But don't get the idea we didn't play hard. We always gave our best.

And somehow, in spite of my apparently incurable appetite for tomfoolery, we were pretty good, too. Our team finished either first or second in the league every year I coached. (And that meaningless fact, along with a couple dollars, will buy you a Mountain Dew most places.)

But my greatest asset was surely not my own coaching ability. I felt it was my ability to surround myself with likeminded assistant coaches. When everyone shares the same philosophy (play hard and have fun) it's easier to accomplish success.

Yet . . . I made mistakes . . . and plenty of 'em.

As was so memorably portrayed in the Paul Newman movie, *Cool Hand Luke,* behind virtually every human conflict the following words can be found to lurk . . . "What we have here is a failure to communicate."

Folks sometimes ask if my teaching the jail inmates is dangerous.

I tell them what's dangerous is umpiring behind home plate in a Little League game.

Most don't take my reply too seriously . . . except for current or former Little League umps, who know very well what I'm talking about!

Just before my first game behind the plate, one parent told me, "Mr. Talley, you'll be a great umpire. All the

parents respect you. You won't have any trouble back
there."

Well, not only did I have trouble, I sometimes had *more*
than the average ump, simply because I knew the parents of
the kids and they felt more comfortable in "letting go" with
me.

In fact, one of the biggest instigators was the very
lady who suggested I become an umpire!

She would stand behind the fence near home plate
and holler things like, "Mr. Talley, it's a good thing you
can teach, 'cause you're a terrible ump."

And she'd hoot, "Boys, there's gonna be a whole heap
of bad calls tonight! Look who's behind the plate, Old Man
Bat Eyes himself. He hears everything . . . but he can't see
a lick!"

I finally asked one of her friends to secretly video her in
full verbal assault, which she managed to do.

Then I mailed the video to Ms. Verbal Assault as a gift,
with a note asking that she sit down and watch it with her
children. I added that she was a good person, and that all
good people made mistakes now and then.

The next game, there she was, standing against the
fence near home plate, ready to hoot and holler, which she
continued to do . . . with all the more unabated gusto than
ever before.

Ms. V. A. let loose at the top of her well-endowed lungs,
"Come on, boys, tonight's a great night! We got a good
man behind the plate. He'll call everything as fair as he
can!"

Then I heard her mumble, just barely loud enough so
that only I could hear, "Even if he can't see a lick."

I turned to look at her. She whispered, "Thank you,"
through the fence. We both grinned ear to ear, but it
was hard to tell whose grin was bigger.

When umpiring behind the plate, I used to call both
teams out of the dugout before the game and tell them, "I'm

going to miss some calls tonight. I just wanted you all to know ahead of time, so you won't be surprised."

Sometimes a kid would ask, "Why?"

My scientifically-oriented mind would reply with something like, "Because I'm human. And part of being human is making mistakes. That's what makes a real umpire better than a robot. Because we're not as good, you never know when a mistake is coming. It keeps the game a lot more exciting … and a lot more like real life."

Sometimes a kid with his thinking cap on would retort, "But the game's not fair, if you make mistakes."

Boy, did I have a good comeback for that line.

I'd bend over, look them straight in the eye and reply, "Little man, whoever in this world ever told you that life was going to be fair?"

Over time, I came to the somewhat regrettable conclusion that fussing and yelling at umpires was just part of baseball Americana. I would bet all my days left on the planet that some fans would scream and yell at Jesus if he donned an umpire mask and called a game behind home plate.

But I never did learn not to take it all quite so personally.

One of my biggest coaching failures was when I failed to properly communicate to one wonderful kid, and his truly good parents, why I was having the boy bunt so much. The kid, previously one of our best hitters, got afraid of the ball and was mired in a terrible slump. He simply couldn't make contact.

But the kid had great speed. So I thought, if I could just get him to bunt, he would likely get on first base and build back his confidence at the same time.

I failed miserably to communicate *why* I was getting him to bunt. To the child and his family, it looked as though I'd "given up" on him. This child, who trusted and esteemed me second only to his parents, quit the team. Then his father lambasted me for embarrassing his kid.

At first, I felt stupefied. For the life of me, I couldn't figure out why they hadn't seen clearly that I was only trying to help this kid overcome his fear of the ball and take a step toward hitting well again.

But, for some reason, I had obviously not communicated this (at all) to this genuinely wonderful family.

I couldn't get the kid to come back.

But apologize, I could do, which I did. I wrote one of the most sincere letters of apology I've ever written (and I've made myself write more than a few of those in my life) to this kid and his entire family.

As virtually always happens when one is sincere and longsuffering, my apology was wholeheartedly accepted . . . and our mutual wounds healed in time. As I said, this was a wonderful family. They were just terribly hurt (however unintentional it may have been on my part) by someone they trusted.

I must say this - apologizing (*especially* when I felt I had *not* committed a wrong) has never appeared to hamper my influence, either as a teacher or a coach. In fact, it has seemed only to enhance respect toward me from those I had (however unintentionally) harmed in some way.

Another time, a mother fussed to high heaven and back again, all over me not starting her son, Simon.

Now her male offspring did well to catch a cold, let alone a baseball. And he likely could miss the backside of a big bull while trying to hit it with a bass fiddle.

Simon was not going to play in the major leagues someday, though Momma seemed to think he was providentially destined to do so.

After a game one day, and right in front of the whole team, Momma gave me the mother of all tongue-lashings.

Well, I decided I'd had enough . . . so I made a mistake.

I asked her to choose one player on our team that she thought should sit out the next game, while her son started.

This lady wasn't unintelligent, however uninformed she may have been about baseball. She refused to pick anyone, knowing she would look very bad to everyone in doing so. So she stomped off . . . madder than ever.

I confess, I thought about having my own son (the league's best hitter and perennial All-Star) sit the bench the next game, but I was keen about being fair to him also. I had seen too many Little League parents coach their own kids and be far too hard on them.

I knew I had to find a way to learn something from this lady.

What would be the most humble, unselfish, yet just, thing to do?

Swallowing pride is much like taking medicine. At first, it tastes terrible, making it easy to spit out. But, if we swallow it whole, as time passes, it begins to heal us from the inside out.

I decided to ask the team to let every player start a game who hadn't done so yet that year. In fact, I asked that the substitutes not only start, but play for at least half the game before we put in the regulars.

Donnie (who had *that* kind of Dad) immediately piped in that we'd lose the game for sure if we played "our scrubs" first.

"Then we'll lose," I replied. "At least, on the scoreboard, we will."

The next game, the scoreboard said we lost. Actually the scoreboard "roared" that we lost. In fact, we lost so badly that the game had to be called early, before our starters could get in and mount a comeback.

After the game, the dugout was quiet. When I asked the boys if they'd learned anything, I got answers that would make a major league manager marvel.

My own son started us off, "I learned that it's okay to lose, if you do it because you're trying to do something bigger than winning."

Simon smiled, "I liked starting for once, but I learned I should look for a college scholarship doing something else."

"Please don't forget to tell that to Momma," I whispered, amidst a flurry of understanding chuckles.

One of the usual starters added, "I learned to put myself in someone else's place. I'm not used to doing that."

And from Donnie (the kid with *that* kind of Dad), "I thought I'd feel terrible, and I did at first. Then in the end I felt kind of good about it. But it was a different type of good than when we win a game."

I quickly replied, "Please don't forget to tell that to your Dad."

This time the chuckles sounded more like a blizzard than a flurry.

A Grandmother's Legacy: Part I

(Dedicated to the Bristol Crisis Center)

To kill . . . or not to kill? That is the question.

I find it more than a bit ironic that a lot of folk, at least in our neck of the woods, will resort to quoting the Bible when *supporting* the death penalty.

Of course, everyone knows that anyone can twist the Bible to prove pretty much anything. It's actually quite an easy thing to do – if you quote the Good Book, however narrow minded your interpretation may be, you may (temporarily, at least) appear to win most arguments.

On close examination, I would maintain that quoting the Bible in support of the death penalty is profoundly and morally self-defeating. I've yet to hear a death penalty supporter tell me that they can reasonably envision Jesus intentionally and premeditatedly murdering another human being.

Because, plain and simple, strapped to the bare bones, that's what capital punishment is – intentional and premeditated murder.

Claiming to be simply following what the law says means nothing from a moral point of view. How many times in history has the "law" been wrong? At present, our nation stands as the only civilized Western country that systematically executes its own citizens in the name of justice.

Of course, some folks, however well-intentioned, harbor an erroneous notion that the death penalty "does good", that it somehow prevents heinous crimes.

Despite many efforts over the years, there has yet to be any widely respected scientific/sociological research to support the somewhat widespread assumption that capital punishment is a deterrent to crime.

So what about the question of "justice"? Shouldn't the perpetrators of particularly heinous acts receive retribution equal to their crime? And aren't there some criminals so horrific (Ted Bundy, Adolf Hitler, etc.), as to have no hope for rehabilitation?

These are fair questions, and one must face them, when seeking an end to premeditated, state-sanctioned murder (euphemistically referred to as "capital punishment").

I would answer these questions with a question at least as fair and perhaps more powerful: *Why do we kill people to show people that killing people is wrong?"*

It doesn't take sociological research to plainly see two other monumental facts related to state-sanctioned murder.

Fact one: Those executed are largely the poor. Think – when was the last time you saw someone with substantial material means gassed, electrocuted, or injected by the state?

Fact two: Countless thousands of those on death row, throughout human history, have ultimately been deemed not guilty *after* their conviction, often only days from death . . . and too many times too late.

Neither of these facts is ever disputed by educated people. Indeed, they are absolutely striking facts in favor of abolishing the death penalty.

Yet, state-sanctioned, premeditated murder still exists in our country. (Yes, I know, some insist on using the less shocking euphemisms "capital punishment" or "death penalty". I prefer to call it what it is.)

Sometimes one hears reasoning offered along these lines: "It saves the state a lot of money to execute, as compared to life in prison". There are two serious problems with this reasoning.

One: If it is indeed morally wrong to execute a fellow human being, as a growing number of informed Americans deem that it is, then it's a moot point.

Slavery was once legal in this country, but that did not make it morally right to own human beings as slaves. My hopes are that we find the courage to measure capital punishment with the same moral compass as we ultimately did slavery.

Two: Even if one succumbs to another standard and refuses to see consider capital punishment as morally wrong, there are still mountainous statistics which counter the argument that its use is somehow a "good" thing.

The short answer is – it costs nearly as much, and sometimes more, to execute as it does to imprison for life (once one computes the massive investigation and litigation expenses, the inevitable process of appeals, and the question of lifespan – since a surprisingly large number of death row inmates die before their execution is ever carried out).

And if one purports that "at least the vast majority of those we execute are guilty, so we should speed up the execution process", one opens Pandora's Box.

All reasonable people must admit that over a period of time many who are innocent will die, as long as we have a death penalty. The chance for human error is always with us.

And is it really worth the lives of countless innocent citizens to "do away with" our worst criminals? Our most fundamental and cherished legal rights fly in the face of this assumption. I think proponents and abolitionists alike would agree that the execution of innocent citizens is anything but just.

So what about the issue of providing "closure" for the families of murder victims?

The sense of "closure" that families are told to expect is often simply nonexistent, as someone else's son or daughter has been killed – supposedly, as the state will tell the family, in "retribution" for their own loss. *(For those with the courage to research further, visit: http://www.ncadp.org/pages/about , but –*

I *must warn you, if you are currently pro-capital punishment, be prepared for a possible life-changing experience.)*

When finally confronted with the powerful reasoning against capital punishment, many supporters will inevitably grow frustrated and state what they deem to be their ultimate "emotive case".

They'll say something like this: "I'm sure you would change your mind if *you* ever have a loved one victimized by an unimaginably horrific crime".

Well, I have.

My own grandmother, a dear lady who cared deeply for everyone in her hometown, was the victim of what some have called Bristol's most heinous crime. You cannot read these words and imagine the terror and torture this innocent lady suffered at the hands of an unfeeling brute for hours on end.

Trust me. You have never seen a movie scene so graphic. You simply cannot imagine, even in your worst nightmares, a happening so savage.

My grandmother had lived peaceably for over half a century in her little green house by the side of the road. That house still stands on the corner of Norfolk Avenue and Mary Street.

One hellish May night, she called. "Help me. I've been raped."

The police arrived just ahead of us. Her blood had been splattered on the walls of every upstairs room of her house. We found her battered, stunned, and dehumanized. No one knows how she survived. She was molested, raped, and beaten for hours on end by a young man who had that very same day been released from the Bristol Jail.

Were my grandmother to die, we were told by the state that the death penalty would have been sought in her case.

Indeed, my grandmother did live on for several years – but only as a shell of her formerly vibrant self, her joyous spirit stripped from her by the most misguided of souls. (That soul is now incarcerated for life without parole.)

Would I personally "pull the switch" on this man who animalized a loved one? Would I feel a sense of justice in committing such an act of violence?

To kill ... or not to kill? That is the question.

I've given it quite a bit of thought over the years. If I may say so, I feel that I've somewhat "earned" the right to make a personal choice on what I consider a spiritual question.

After examining all of the evidence on "both sides" quite thoroughly, I've come to the long-pondered conclusion that the choice of who lives and who dies is best left up to a Greater Power than human courts.

Even in our best and most honorable attempts at justice, we are too often wrong.

And where death is concerned, there are no second chances at being right.

A Grandmother's Legacy: Part II

"Come over here," said my grandmother. "We're going to write that fellow a letter."

Grandmothers are usually the first to notice any change in their grandchildren.

For quite a while now, I'd not been laughing as much. And for me, that was a big change.

The trouble was, I knew what my grandmother meant by "that fellow". It was the phrase she always used when referring to the young man who had so savagely assaulted her a few months before.

"Mamaw, we can't do that. He'll just show your letter around in prison and make fun of it."

"Go get me my Bible," she said.

I did as my grandmother asked.

"Now open it," she continued, "and show me where it says we're not supposed to forgive people."

"But Mamaw, this guy is not human. He's worse than an animal. He's nothing but a big mistake."

My grandmother was undaunted. "Well then, open my Bible and show me where it says God makes some people by mistake."

Mamaw had me and she knew it.

"Okay, I'll help you write it."

It went something like this:

"You are right where you're supposed to be. You ruined the last years of my life and brought a terrible hurt on the lives of all my family. But I want you to know that I forgive you. Maybe God has something special for you where you are."

I told her I'd mail it.

But she was too wise for that.

"Promise me," she said, "that you won't just mail it, but that you'll see that it gets mailed to the exact person and exact address it needs to go to."

I hesitated. "But Mamaw, I just don't see what good this is going to do for anybody."

"You go and do what your Mamaw tells you, okay? I raised my family better than that. Now do you promise to get this letter to that fellow?"

I had only one answer.

I mailed the letter the next day.

We never heard back from "that fellow".

As a couple of weeks passed, I began to sense that Mamaw never really expected to.

Meanwhile, I found myself laughing a lot again. I felt more at peace than I had at any time since Mamaw's diabolical ordeal.

Then it hit me like a slab of cold ice on a hot day.

I had to go see Mamaw … and tell her.

As soon as she saw me come to the door, I knew that she knew.

And she knew that I knew she knew.

"Mamaw," I said. "You didn't write that letter for that fellow, now, did you?"

She smiled.

"And you didn't write it for yourself, either."

She smiled again.

"Mamaw, you wrote that letter for *me*. I had to let go of all the hate - and you helped me."

I could hardly hold back tears.

"Now, now," she said. "I've been thinkin' a lot. And I believe you might be called to go help the folks down at the city jail."

Mamaw proved to be a prophet.

In time, I began my dual work as a Good News Jail and Prison volunteer and as the men's GED instructor at the Bristol Jail.

It's been thirty years now . . . and I feel my grandmother with me every time I look into an inmate's face. Being human, I still occasionally get angry at people, but I never look at anyone with hate. No, not anymore . . . no matter what. My grandmother raised her family better than that.

Discovering the Real Mayberry

(In honor and memory of my mother, Helen Talley ...
the real-life Aunt Bee)

Some folks still wish for Mayberry, the town that actually never was (at least as portrayed on the popular television show).

However, there remains a very real connection to the mythical Mayberry that we can each reclaim daily.

The simple act of writing a personal note or letter will do it. This time-honored act somehow serves to revive within our souls the nostalgic pleasures of long ago, small-town America. Yes, indeed, the simple penning of a note to a friend can soothe our homesick yearnings for yesteryear.

I swear to Aunt Bee, it's even better than watching a rerun of Andy and Barney at their finest.

I actually *like* to write letters and notes. I always have.

I like to write to the young man at the fast food window who is extra nice in handling my order.

Or I may leave an encouraging note to the lady (named Juanita or not) at one of our local diners whose feet pound miles daily so her children can dream for their future each night.

Often I write these type of letters anonymously, as there appears to be a hidden power in doing good deeds quietly. Humility carries more strength than pride ever knew.

I like to write to the police officer who writes me a ticket. He or she is daily subjected to public criticism (much like Deputy Fife), yet too rarely receives a kind "thank you" for keeping our community safe.

I like to write to children (like Opey) who have every-day needs.

I like to write to jail inmates (like Otis) who truly suffer behind their mask of self-abuse.

I like to write to parents (like Andy) who occasionally feel like failures.

I'll have my current students write letters to service men and women in our armed forces, whom I previously taught as children.

Yes, even (and maybe especially) the ones who remind me of Gomer.

One previous student responded to our letters by visiting with us when in on leave from Iraq. As a gift, he brought to us a huge American flag that had once flown over his desert base camp for months.

To this flag we have ever since pledged our allegiance each morning in school.

Over the years, we've had a varied assortment of guest speakers visit my classroom from all walks of life; mayors, senators, armed service personnel, doctors, lawyers, plumbers, janitors, florists, and karate teachers have all ventured our way.

We even once invited a barber. (No, I can't say his name was Floyd.)

To each we always took the time to deliver a personalized letter.

Years ago, we had inmate pen-pals, which was a huge hit for families of children and inmates alike. (In today's litigious-minded culture, this one might be a bit harder to pull off. But I can tell you without reservation, if done right - with the children remaining anonymous and with me proofing all letter traffic in and out - this endeavor brought more visible joy to both parties than any other pen-pal undertaking I can ever recall.)

The children and I create get-well cards for those among us who have relatives in the hospital . . . and sympathy cards for those who've lost a loved one.

In this age of instant, distant communication, a personally handwritten note, card, or letter is all the more valued and appreciated.

My own octogenarian mother (yes, indeed, she does remind many folks of Aunt Bee) had a lifetime "note ministry" of such. She spent a large part of each day painfully, but ever joyously, handwriting notes of encouragement to all the sick, just married, graduated, and bereaved people she could find on the planet.

Some may say that her efforts, when balanced against the world itself, were a small task.

I fancy those thankful souls who've found themselves on the receiving end of her countless notes and letters would disagree quite heartily with such a statement.

Myself, I cordon off a late twenty minutes to a half hour each and every night for such activity. When one doesn't miss a night, this little labor of love can produce exponential results.

I must also admit, such a labor can lose its love and morph into a painstaking duty. At such times, all I need do is simply have the will and faith to begin the task . . . and the sheer act of note writing itself reminds me of why I do it. I often finish with a sense of fulfillment not easily found elsewhere.

My hopes are that we, each in our own way, seek to bring back this little touch of Mayberry generally thought headed toward extinction.

We can all do our part to write at least one simple, heartfelt letter each day. We can revive this lost art.

The simple act of handwritten communication to a fellow human being – it goes a long way toward bringing back a little touch of small-town America.

And remember . . . a real Mayberry there never was.

But a real Bristol, there is. And if you think about it, that reality makes it even *better* than the fictional Mayberry.

Bristol, it's for real . . . and it's a good place to live.

So good, in fact, that we should write each other about it.

The Visiting of Humble Abodes

(Dedicated to the Haven of Rest Rescue Mission and the
Salvation Army, and everywhere such places exist to help the poor)

Growing up in Bristol my family never locked our
car doors.

Nope, not our house doors either.

Perhaps it's because we knew our neighbors so well. If
letter writing is the lost "art" of small town America,
then I would offer that visiting is the lost "heart".

The first decade and a half I taught, I managed to visit
the home of every single student at least once during the
school year. Then I began to teach over one hundred kids
each year and missed a few, a fact for which I am ever
remorseful.

But I still visit the vast majority during most
years and manage to make it to all homes in others.

My just-drop-by, friendly home visits are always
positive, and never with the intention to "tell" on a child
for something. One reason I am so often invited into homes
may be that I come eager to share with the family good
things I've discovered about their child, things which they
may not even have yet recognized.

Over the years, I've been graciously welcomed into the
homes of princes and paupers alike, so to speak.

Early in my career I visited Ronnie … whose mother
met me at the door with a double-barreled shotgun.

You see, Ronnie's Ma had heard that Ronnie's Pa's
brother's friend (whom no one in the family had yet met)
was coming to talk to Pa, who lay drunk as a skunk
stretched out in the living room floor.

It seems that Ronnie's Pa's brother's friend was
coming to talk Pa about "makin' some money makin'
meth" (which was

not a completely unheard of part-time occupation in this particular poverty-stricken area of town).

But since Ma didn't know Ronnie's Pa's brother's friend's face from Adam, and since Ma had never before laid eyes on me, Ma immediately mistook me for this particular fellow whom she'd never before seen.

Ma had been told by a street-wise informant, "He always wears an Indiana Jones style hat."

Well, exactly such a hat happens to don the perch of yours truly virtually every time I leave my house. When I'm not teaching school, the hat can be found atop my head about ninety-seven percent of my waking life.

Staring down two barrels, I (somewhat) calmly asked Ma to holler into the back room and send out her offspring Ronnie to identify yours truly as her child's friendly local pedagogue.

Ma obliged my request. "If my boy says you're his teacher, you're welcome to step over Pa and eat a bite of supper with us. If he don't, then you'd best turn around quick, as buckshot might hurt a bit less diggin' it out of your back end than your front."

The familiar thumping gait of Ronnie romping down the hallway greeted my ears like a sweet symphony.

He called out as he came down the hallway, "Ma, I recognize Mr. T.'s voice already. You can hide shotgun!"

I would have celebrated at once, even before laying eyes on Ronnie's cherubic face . . . but I gave pause to remember the extremely low correlation between human intelligence and people who point shotguns at others.

Turns out, I had a right to pause.

As soon as he turned the corner, Ronnie stopped and stared straight at me with his blankest stare (oh, yes, I'd seen that same blank stare in class many times before).

Then Ronnie muttered, "Ma, I ain't so sure that's Mr. T. 'cause I ain't never seen him wear no hat like that in class!" (Yes, the light was a bit dim in the hallway, but … "Lordamighty", Ronnie!)

At which words Ma happily raised again both barrels and cried, "Listen you, my husband's brother's friend! You'd best not let the front door hit you in the rear, or buckshot will!"

I hadn't been timed in the forty-yard dash since high school. At the last raise of Ma's gun, I fancy I would have timed a personal best. An extra thirty some years and thirty-five pounds are no handicap to a man fleeing the wrath of an ignorant-to-the-bone-so-eager-to-use-shotgun Ma.

As I turned to make a leap off the front porch, it seems I flew out from beneath my hat.

I could hear Ronnie call out, "Ma, put down shotgun! It really is Mr. Talley. I can see his bald head now a-shinin' in the sunlight on porch."

Ma skeddadled onto the front porch alongside Ronnie and called out, "Mr. Talley, I apologize! You come on back up here right now and eat a bite of supper with us. I was just gettin' ready to take it up off stove."

That skillet full of fried baloney and week-old bread was mighty tasty, I must say. In spite of Ma's incessant swatting of the flies (who tried to share the baloney), I can say that I've rarely been treated better at any home I ever visited (discounting the moments prior to my hat falling off).

As I prepared to leave after supper, Ronnie retrieved my hat from the door knob where he'd carefully hung it. I stood in the doorway, my hat perched again on the sphere of its rightful owner, when Pa finally made some sounds as if to revive himself from his inebriated state on the floor.

When Pa came to, he sat up and stared me straight in the face. It was a look much like Ronnie had given me a thousand times in the classroom. (The apple does not fall far from the tree.)

"Ma, grab shotgun!" Pa screamed. "It's my brother Bill's friend. I can tell by his hat!"

Yet again I felt an urge to test my speed in the forty, when I heard little Ronnie gleefully chirp, "Mr. Talley, stay and watch Ma bang Pa up side head with skillet!"

I had already turned toward the doorway, when I heard a loud hollow clang behind me, followed in about three seconds by a deadening thud … then a muted female voice muttering, "Drunken fool".

When I dared peep back around, my eyes were cast upon the aftermath of Ma's skill with skillet. A properly swung frying pan from Ma had returned Pa to his previous state of stupor. He lay prostrate on the living room floor. All this while Ronnie reached for another piece of fly-enriched fried baloney.

Judging by the reaction of Ronnie when Ma connected with Pa, a flailing by Ma of Pa with skillet was not an uncommon occurrence in this household … probably about as often as swatting flies off fried baloney.

...

In visiting the homes of my students, I've discovered one overriding and reassuring fact: in spite of the wide variance in the size and style of their abodes … people love to make guests feel right at home.

One student's grandparents invited me inside their multi-million dollar mansion to gorge on ten-dollar-a-bite steak and caviar.

I had stopped by to say "Hi" and brag on their grandchild. I came wearing my customary attire - jeans, hiking boots, and (of course) my trademark hat.

To these good people, it didn't matter if I came dressed as Blackbeard. I seriously doubt if a king or a president would have been treated with more self-respect and dignity. The fact that I happened by while this family was in the midst of throwing a big party for business clients meant nothing to them. They made me feel as if I were worth a billion dollars.

With equal aplomb, I've shared scraps fresh from a fast food dumpster with a family living in an abandoned nearby barn.

Which was the better meal I've mentioned thus far ... the steak and caviar, the fried baloney and flies, or the dumpster food?

I reckon I'd have to rate them all about even. Virtually any meal shared among friends feels like a five star banquet.

There seems to be a disturbing misunderstanding in America – that people don't want visitors just dropping in. I've found quite the contrary to be true – people are starving for just-drop-by friendly visits.

One must only be mindful to stay a brief time and be positive while there. From my personal experience, these are the conditions that have enabled me to both give and receive a joy which costs no money and knows no bounds. Visit someone today in their humble abode. Don't stay too long. Just drop by to say "Hi". Ask how everyone is doing and act like you care ... because you really do.

Keeping the Personal Touch

(Dedicated to Girls Inc. of Bristol)

One of the greatest blessings of living in a little Appalachian town like ours is that you can get to know people around you. And not just know who they are, but know them *personally*.

Our loss of a sense of community, most social scientists tell us, is a root cause of many modern mental illnesses. In the words of one prominent psychologist, "Many people now feel detached from others, with a sinking feeling that life is passing them by."

A sense of community is much of what helps us lead meaningful lives.

And even in a good old town like ours, that sense of community can always be nourished to grow even stronger.

At the end of each school year I give each student a penny. The penny is taped to a letter, which reads something like this: *Keep this penny and guard it like the treasure it is, for it represents your education.*

The letter goes on to tell each child to mail it to me when they graduate high school and I'll mail them ten dollars in return.

I look forward to receiving these pennies every month of May. If the children stay in our school system, as most do, I simply hand out the ten dollar bills the night of their graduation ceremony at the high school.

So far I've received pennies from as far away as California, Germany, and Australia. Kids don't often forget if they value something enough.

Every once in a while, I've had well-intentioned folk tell me that some of what I do is too "personal", that I should not be so "involved" in the lives of my students.

I know of no other way to do what I do. Most of what I do with my students is "personal" in some form or fashion.

I have strong evidence that it's not the literal ten dollars which my students most value, or even the penny itself. Indeed, it's not unusual for a student to try to refuse accepting the ten dollars from me. It appears what they cherish most is the personal communication connection that the "penny promise" affords us to maintain over the years.

I'll receive an occasional note, phone call, or email (and nowadays, of course, text messages) from previous students who tell me they've lost their penny.

I tell them not to worry. I tell them that the fact that they cared enough to contact me makes the penny "reappear", even if they no longer can see it.

I've found that lavish gifts are unnecessary to show we care. In fact, my experience watching parents has taught me that expensive gifts often work to the contrary, spoiling children and buying everything but personal time, which is what children really crave most.

Too often, even in this good town, I've found that some parents come close to drowning their children with a desire for material things (yes, even the poor can do this).

One of the fondest times of my life was one lazy Saturday afternoon when my grandchildren and I lay on our backs in a field. We had originally intended to spend the day doing things together that would require spending money left and right.

Instead, we passed the time blowing dandelions, counting butterflies, and finding shapes in the drifting clouds. They had my full time and complete attention, without spending a dime. And I dare say they still remember that day with at least as much glee as any hundred dollar day at a theme park.

"Popaw!" squealed one of my grandchildren. I forget whether it was Allie or Aaron. "This is the most funnest day we have yet lived."

Whatever the gift, I like to make it small in cost, but large in personalized meaning.

People the world over are practically screaming and begging for more personal communication, something that each of us can give. Not to totally discard the new ways, for some modern technology has its clear advantages, but to revive in each of us a bit more of what makes us human . . . the personal touch.

Take personal chances. Make personal visits. Write personal notes. Forgive personally. Get involved personally. Do it now.

To Live By

(Dedicated to all who worship as they feel led by freedom of conscience, the greatest of our American rights: whether it be in a church, synagogue, temple, mosque, ashram, sanctuary, or shrine ... or simply by doing good toward the Earth and their fellow man)

The following words were inspired by the character of the good bishop found in the beginning of Victor Hugo's masterpiece, *Les Miserables*, perhaps my favorite novel. Because of its enormous length, few attempt to read every page. Yet those who do invest the time come away recompensed for a lifetime.

Someday I would like to live this way. I strive to do so now. Yet, as the reader well knows, things get in the way of our noblest intentions. Perhaps the reader will strive along with me . . .

Live simply.
Give hope and warmth as you go.
Treat every soul as your own.
Live humbly.
Laugh a lot.
Write and visit often.
Treat both poor and rich the same – both need love.
Fight ignorance not with darkness, but with light.
Marvel at the stars.
Play with children.
Hold grudges against no one.
Think deeply.
Walk daily in the fields and woods.
Stay learned and well-read.
Above all, be compassionate and forgiving.

It'll Tickle Yore Innards

(Dedicated to the Rotary Club of Bristol)

The Mountain Dew people owe me money. I don't really know how much, but they don't have enough in the bank to pay me for all the free advertising I've done for them with children over the years.

Actually, come to think of it, they've done a lot for me too. They just don't know about it.

Seems I got addicted to Mountain Dew at about age four.

My family stopped at a little store in Marion, Virginia, on our way to camp at Hungry Mother State Park. My Dad handed my big sister a green glass bottle through our open back seat car window.

"Try a swig of this new drink," Dad said.

The bottle had a caricature of a hillbilly saying something on it. Big Sis told me the hillbilly was hollerin', "It'll tickle yore innards!"

Big Sis took one swig and told me I could have all the rest if I liked it. "Don't be afraid to try it," she told me.

Little Brother's first swig on the bottle has since turned into millions. It was love at first taste. Mountain Dew and I would forever after be connected at the lip.

My students figured it out recently. At two Dews a day, on average (for those who know me, this is a conservative daily estimate), since I was first smitten with Dewitis . . . well, that'd be 2 x 365 x 56 (years) = 40,880 Dews total. Then multiply by 12 to get total ounces (although many a time I've been seen turning up a 16 ouncer, or more).

If my students' savvy calculations are correct, I've likely swigged more than half a million ounces of Dew in my lifetime.

Will my kidneys and liver make it to a million? Time will tell.

We all have our bad habits. Maybe I'll break this one before it finally breaks me. Time will tell.

Of course, I've used Mountain Dew as a reward quite often in the classroom. Giving children little tangible things is fine, as long as we inch them toward an understanding that life's best rewards are intangible and cost not a nickel.

Like their teacher (and perhaps, *because* of their teacher), I've found that my students will do almost anything for a chance to swig down a Mountain Dew. Evidently the original hillbilly caption remains true to this day. The Dew ever retains its remarkable ability to "tickle yore innards".

For instance, if the entire class is able to answer a specified number of questions correctly, we might have a drawing for a prize … and everyone knows what the prize might be.

But the prize/reward isn't always Mountain Dew.

The reward might be the chance to stand on a desk and quack like a duck (yes, it's amazing to some that children are eager to do this, if it's seen as a reward for doing something good).

Instead of a Dew, a child might win a chance to run outside our classroom, hug a tree, and return singing God Bless America.

In lieu of a Dew, someone might win a chance to go with me on a Saturday hike, or to write one of my GED students at the jail a letter of encouragement (anonymously, of course), or simply to walk around the room for three minutes, while shaking everyone's hand and saying in their best Australian accent, "Good day, mate!"

The list of these types of rewards I have for children is endless and ever evolving. Notice that the rewards, though all "fun", are often a service toward others. (So even the act of giving a Dew is not as pointless as it may seem at face value. There is always, if one looks a bit wider and deeper, a method to be found behind the madness.)

The only reward that actually costs me money is giving away Mountain Dew as a prize.

By the way, I was once mysteriously struck with momentary insanity and swore off Mountain Dew for a while (with the honorable intention of being a better health role model for the kids).

This lapse of good hillbilly reason lasted might nigh a month, before I got off the wagon and got back to being myself again (faults and all).

. . .

Earlier in my career, I was visiting the middle school early one morning. I noticed a couple of teachers pointing toward me and laughing as I passed them in the hall. Their laughter contained a hinted tone of derision – the one type of laughter you don't want thrown your way.

So I stopped to ask them how I'd made their day.

They blushed and told me they had just come from a behavioral conduct meeting with one of my former elementary school students. This particular student had been raised on the streets of New York City, but had moved here to Bristol a couple of years earlier. The student, now in middle school, was at the meeting, along with his grandmother who raised him.

The ladies could hardly contain their guffawing, as they tried to tell me what had transpired to inspire their burst of frivolity at my expense.

It seems that everyone around the table was trying to come up with a behavioral consequence/reward system for Leon. But Leon was consistently rejecting every potential reward they came up with, no matter how good they tried to make it for him.

Then they told me Leon's grandmother finally piped up and in. "Glory hallelujah!" she hollered. "I've got the answer. Mr. Talley used to drive by on the weekend when Leon had a good week and drop him off a Mountain Dew. Leon be good as gold for that!"

Leon evidently brightened up at this point . . . but not the teachers. Even with the grandmother plainly stating the way to Leon's heart, the meeting adjourned for lack of a consensus on how to help Leon.

These two otherwise good ladies remained unenlightened as to the method behind my "madness". I was operating on the old premise that people don't care how much you know until they know how much you care.

Mountain Dew was not the "reward" so prized by Leon. Respect was. But only those with eyes to look past the superficial could see it. And not everyone has such vision. It was quite obvious that my two compatriots had made their minds up to see only what they desired to see. Their vision, however sharp, was extremely narrow in scope. Certainly, we are all guilty of such fixated tunnel-vision at times in our lives.

But back to me in the hallway … once I got the gist of what happened, I quickly asked the two, "Where's Leon now?"

"He just went downstairs and back to class."

I couldn't even begin to hold a grudge against these two ladies. (Holding grudges may be the most "unproductive" force known to mankind.)

I sprinted down the stairs and leaped around the corner, catching a glimpse of Leon just before he entered a classroom.

I called out for him.

Leon rushed over to give me his most special type of "brother" handshake and hug, which, I'd learned was preserved for use with only a chosen, trusted few.

"My man, Mr. T., we just been talkin' 'bout you!" I only had a few seconds, so my words had to be succinct

"Do what's right the rest of this week, Leon, and I'll visit you with a surprise this weekend."

Leon smiled and spoke in his rhythmical inner-city vernacular. "It ain't gonna be no surprise, Mr. T., I already know what it gonna be. I gotcha covered on this end. See you dis weekend, man."

Leon never gave me a Mountain Dew in return. Not even once.

He didn't have to.

Leon's return gift to me was something much more lasting and tasty. Because he knew I cared, he gave me the greatest reward of which he was capable.

Respect ... it'll tickle yore innards. Maybe even better than . . .

Naah, I just can't say it ... at least not before I taste another sip.

The Appalachian Trail

(as told by son David, at age fifteen)

(Dedicated to all Boy and Girl Scout troops in our region)

I begin walking the Appalachian Trail from Hwy. 421 at the very top, just before you go down into Shady Valley.

Dad lets me off here. But he's driving on down through Shady Valley and up to the Carter County line to begin his hike.

We each walk the Appalachian Trail, but he travels north as I hike south. We plan to meet somewhere in between, at the Trail shelter on Holston Mountain.

Dad told me to look to my right as I walk further along the crest of the mountain and I might catch some glimpses of Bristol far below.

I'm probably hoofing it a little faster than I normally would, because I have the longer distance to travel to meet up with Dad. Besides, I don't want to be late because we're going to eat at the house of Mr. Marler (a teacher friend of Dad's) tonight … and I'm going to help him cook!

At one point I pass some old folks (all even older than Dad) coming down the ridge.

I also see a lot of different types of birds on the first part of my hike. I can't tell if they are migrating already or just fattening up to get ready.

I am probably a bit too fast to see much else, though I enjoy every step. I notice the further in elevation I go up, the more the leaves are already showing color.

I pause in one big clearing to search for White Top and Mount Rogers, the two tallest mountains in Virginia, back behind me. I barely make them out through the haze. It's a beautiful day with more than a hint of autumn tinging the air, but hazy in the distance.

When I look down to my right beyond blue South

Holston Lake, and through certain little gaps in the colored leaves, I see it. I catch a couple of murky glimpses of a town far below.

It must be Bristol.

I know Holston Mountain is not quite as tall or as rocky-topped as Grandfather Mountain in North Carolina, which Dad and I hiked straight up from the base this past summer. But Dad says Holston is probably longer because it stretches nearly forty miles from Damascus to near Elizabethton. He says if you hike the backbone of Holston Mountain on a clear winter's day, Bristol stays in sight down below most of the way.

I get to the Appalachian Trail shelter ahead of Dad and wait for a few minutes, then decide to go on and meet him coming up from the opposite way. We meet in about one minute after I started down.

Dad had just seen a bear cub, not five minutes before. He shows me exactly where on the way down. It had run across his path, climbed a tree, skittered right back down, then hypered on over the ridge. Of course, we keep two eyes out for Mom, just in case she happens to come ask us if we've seen Junior.

Lots of really large ferns spurt up alongside this part of the Appalachian Trail near the top, giving this section kind of a tropical look.

Further down, we spy many sprouted up mushrooms. They look to be greeting Dad and me from side to side.

As we near the bottom quarter of our hike, the cicadas decide they should begin serenading us. I see one in the path enduring its last death throes before returning to the soil (or a nocturnal scavenger's belly).

We break into the open meadow/farmland, which covers nearly the last full mile of our hike. We imagine Momma Bear bursting forth from the woods behind us . . . and us running down the meadow! We each welcome a shiver down our spines. We made it seem as if it were a real occurrence when we ran.

Lots of ironweed and goldenrod abound all around in this high mountain meadow.

We pause to eat apples from an old apple tree, whose ancestors were likely planted by a now-long-gone settler. This area reminds me of Hensley Settlement atop Cumberland Mountain on the Misha Mokwa Scout Trail, back when I hiked it with Boy Scout Troop 3 from First Presbyterian Church in Bristol.

I use to talk about building a cabin someday in a place like this, but now I've decided it would ruin the whole view. I'll just come up here and sit and enjoy it like it is.

Dad said he hoped that I would always take the time to hike alone in my life regularly, to think deeply and freely about things. Nature has a way of allowing that, like nothing else can.

Wow . . . how one hike up here can change your whole view of things down below!

Or maybe it was all those hikes from years before that added up - and this one finally brought out a change in me. I'm not sure.

But I'm sure I'll always do this – walk in the wild - as a part of my life.

They call it the Appalachian Trail. But it's not just for people here. It's for people the world over. I wish they all knew what they were missing.

Haunted Forests, Deaf-Mutes and Headless Horsemen

(Dedicated to United Way of Bristol)

We call it the Black Forest for good reason. If you dare to venture through it on a moonless night, you can't see your hand in front of your face.

The Black Forest is the perfect venue for our Haunted Forest tours, which we offer to hundreds of kids near Halloween each year. It's a special time for children to learn how to face down their fears.

I take turns sauntering small groups, or "tours", along a narrow half-mile trail that leads through a huge grove of evergreens at Sugar Hollow Park.

The Black Forest was one of many trails initially marked by my son, David, for the first Eagle Scout project done in the park. Hence, we've now had several Eagle Scouts complete their projects at Sugar Hollow.

But back to the Haunted Forest tours … former students of mine, now in high school or college, leap out at opportune times to mortify the wits out of the little waifs who waltz by in the darkness.

The big kids get quite creative in frightening the smaller ones, although about all it actually takes to do so is leaping out from behind a tree while donning a scary mask.

Anything like falling into hidden slime pits or running through fake spider webs are mere bonuses. So are self-opening coffins and a myriad of creepy sound effects.

Those high school and college kids can get quite creative.

Of course, no harm is done and the children are thrilled by this type of fright – because they're at that marvelous age when they can learn how to separate fact from fantasy.

The children naturally love helping each other through the Haunted Forest – and I always give "extra points" to each group that gets through with neither a scratch nor complaint.

If the kids are too scared to move, which actually sometimes happens, they can simply enjoy the campfires we build in raised fire pits on the walkway near one end of the trail.

One Haunted Forest night we found a beggar living in a cave.

This was back when I owned land behind the Bristol, Tennessee Wal-Mart, in the Sunnybrook subdivision. Many wooded acres stood there, adorned with forty-five trails (all created by yours truly with the help of children) of various lengths and topography. It was a child's paradise.

One particular Halloween I talked a parent into portraying a homeless deaf-mute individual, who supposedly lived at the mouth of the cave on this property. (On many another day, the children and I have traversed deep into this naturally wild cave, eventually winding up directly beneath the Wal-Mart.)

That particular year, on our tour of the Haunted Woods, I paused at the mouth of the cave each time, spellbindingly allowing the deaf-mute to appear. I told each tour party, children and parents alike, that the poor deaf-mute ate the moss growing on the side of the cave entrance to stay alive. (Each group had already been instructed to bring along scraps of food left over from our campfire supper. As always, I was striving to instill kindness within the children, which was the higher purpose of this prank, above all else.)

As everyone arrived at the mouth of the cave, they tossed their scraps out there. Soon the deaf-mute made himself seen, peering back and waving gratefully.

Well, lo and behold, at the end of my third tour, here came a parent with blankets and groceries.

"I ran over to Wal-Mart and bought these for that poor deaf-mute," she announced, then asked who would help her distribute the items.

I didn't have the heart to tell the kind lady that the deaf-mute was really just another parent. It would embarrass her in front of everyone else.

So I just let her carry on. It didn't matter, because everyone else there, parent and child alike, thought the deaf-mute was authentic too!

Perhaps the deaf-mute and I should have received nominations for Academy Award performances that night.

At another Haunted Forest behind my old homeplace, another so-willing-to-help parent donned the full attire of the legendary Headless Horseman of Sleepy Hollow fame.

This included the riding of a real live horse ... a real big black live horse.

Of course, I talked up the legend for the better part of an hour before dark, all the while edging the children ever closer to the cave, from whence I predicted the Horseman would make his appearance at the very coming of dusk.

The children peered and squinted and gawked down toward the cave. If anyone looked away, even for an instant, I was quick to redirect their gaze. "You must look toward the cave," I insisted, "Or you'll miss your once chance to see the Headless Horseman!"

Suddenly we heard the pounding of hooves. Everyone turned around to see the Headless Horseman riding straight toward us *from behind*. With a jack-o-lantern head raised high in one hand, it was clear to us all that he had no head above his shoulders.

There was no escape. Our backs now faced toward the cave.

The Horseman galloped up so close that some could feel the breath of his steed ... or so they later claimed.

The Horseman hurled his jack-o-lantern head toward our feet. Then he faded away back into the black as quickly as he had come, having seared his brief visit into our memories for a lifetime.

Science "Prediction Game" for All-Day Sugar Hollow Field Trip: 125 Children

(Also known as: Yes, Appalachian Children Are as Smart as Any)

(To be read and completed by each student prior to our upcoming hike)

(Dedicated to the Bristol Parks and Recreation Department)

Before Sugar Hollow Dam was built, downtown Bristol was often flooded by Beaver Creek. But can you name what other good this dam might do, besides control floods?

I've seen many a Great Blue Heron catching fish in front of the dam, as the fish flop tumbling out into a whirlpool along their journey from beneath. Why might herons find it easier to catch fish here than on the other side of the dam, where the water is calm?

Up the hill to the Old Preston Place, to see three things: a walnut tree, wild wheat in a meadow, and "hitchhikers" – a type of weed whose seeds stick to your clothing for a free ride. Mr. Talley will lay all three things in the road for you to see as you pass by (don't touch, just look). Predict whether you think everyone will listen or not.

At the peak of the hill we enter a pine forest. Look for woodpecker holes on two trees to your left. What was the woodpecker eating? What animals might now live in the woodpecker holes?

Nearing the first bridge, you'll see a cave den off to your right. What kind of rock are caves made from? Why is it "soft" for a rock?

Cross the first of many bridges you will cross today.

What kind of rock (layered, like cake) is that you see just after crossing the bridge?

We now enter the wetlands. Why do you think you might find more bird poop on the bridges here than anywhere else?

Place a check mark over which of the following animals you think may live here in these wetlands: raccoons, frogs, squirrels, turtles, deer, wolves, owls, mosquitoes, foxes, spiders, salamanders, and ducks. Now go back and circle the animals on your list which hibernate for the winter. Do any of them migrate?

As we move on, look for wildflowers . . . and the two towering sycamore trees to your right. Estimate their height: _____. The sycamores have scaly bark, which you can see peeling off. Sycamore trees only grow near a lot of water.

The late summer drought will keep you from seeing this wetland filled with water, as it should be. All that wavy grass you see near the bridges should be covered with water. Why do you think some adults are afraid to admit that global climate change (often called global warming) is as real as the air they breathe? Are you ever afraid of a truth that scares you?

Look for the twin "climbing" sycamore trees to your left. Do you think my son once climbed twenty feet up into one of these trees?

Look for algae covered water to your right. What are the microscopic creatures which live in stagnant water called? What great purpose do algae serve? What all does the algae need for photosynthesis (to make its own food)?

Now cross a bridge with running water. Why is this water more "drinkable" than stagnant water?

Do you see the "squirrel and raccoon proof" birdhouses?

Leave the wetlands now and enter the deciduous hardwood forest. Look at the brightly colored trees around you. What is it that trees lose from their leaves to reveal their true colors? What do we call it when these trees "fall asleep" for the winter?

Look at the soil here. Is it dark and filled with humus? Or light and filled with clay?

Look for dead logs decaying. What new life does their death bring to the forest?

Be careful on this part of the path. There is a groundhog burrow right in the middle of the path. Don't twist an ankle. I hear he barks at boys and whistles at girls as they pass by. What other animals might live in this burrow once the groundhog leaves (or barks and whistles himself to death)?

Now it's on to the picnic shelters. But . . . don't eat yet. Lunch will taste better after you've seen what's next.

Notice the manmade rock wall along the creek near the first shelter. Look for the water snails, the spiral-shelled predictors of relatively clean streams in the Appalachian Mountains. Estimate how many you'll see in the stream here, if you look closely: a few, dozens, hundreds, thousands, ten thousand or more? (Hint: it may surprise you.)

Cross over Water Snake Bridge and enter a slightly different forest along the Cascade Trail. What is a cascade? Will you find acorns in a hardwood forest?

Look for tree carvings on the beech tree trunks (those trees with extra smooth bark) all along this trail. If one carving says "1888", then how old is it, if it is authentic? How could we tell whether the carving is authentic?

Look for a fallen tree, sawed in two, with a new burrow beneath it. We must cross almost directly over this burrow. Why will a skunk *not* likely come out now, if it lives here?

Look at the two big beech trees to the left of this burrow. They appear to have the "mumps". Can plants catch diseases too? What two parts does a plant cell have, which an animal cell does not?

A fallen tree crosses the creek here. Mr. T. and twenty children saw a big ol' bear walk over this bridge this past summer (no, it wasn't Mr. T.). We'll walk over this bridge Saturday, but not today. Think . . . why not today?

On we go. Look for the old farm fencerow to your left. Did the people who built it have a Food City or a McDonald's? Yet in what ways might life have been better for them?

Then ... listen. See if you can be the first to hear it – the sound of falling water. Think of sound waves and how they would "show" the sound of falling water.

Several old fallen logs cross the creek on ahead. Do you see water-skeeters walking on the water here? How are these insects *adapted* to stay afloat on water? (Draw what you think a water-skeeter may look like.)

Now it's up a steep cliff. Stay low here. Why is it best not to stand up too straight? Why do you think a bald-headed old man can climb this hill as well, or better than, any kid at Van Pelt?

We'll cross under a wild "swinging vine" after we reach the top. Mr. T. once swung a kid plum from here into next week on this vine. The kid (named Jimmy Cheers, who now is part owner of a mountain sports business) came back and told us it was going to be partly cloudy on Monday and rain a bit on Tuesday. He was right.

But . . . since we now have the Weather Channel to predict our weather, I won't be swinging anyone else. Was the kid just lucky, or did he really predict the weather (since it came true)? Think like a scientist.

Next up, see if you can find the remains of Big Jim's baby's bed along the left side of the path. Do you see the rusty old coiled springs of the bed? What simple machine is the coiled spring?

We backtrack just a bit here. See if you can notice anything different from when you came up the Cascade Trail. Is winter any closer than when you first started today? Are the days growing longer or shorter? What causes our four seasons?

Over Crawdad Bridge (in single file, remember). I seine here with kids in the summer. What does "seine" mean?

Why are the rocks smooth in the creek? What does muddy water do to life in the creek?

Touch the big limestone boulder on the right. Is its mass more, or less, than your car, if they have the same perimeter measurements? What caused the perfectly circular hole in the big rock? By the way, which weighs more – a ton of feathers or a ton of rocks?

Remember the big ol' bear that crossed the fallen tree bridge? Well, look for his fur stuck along the rocks and roots here. Looks like he had an itch somewhere that he just couldn't seem to scratch!

I suppose the bear could have made use of the sycamore tree you see here, which just happens to have a shape like a natural commode near its base.

LUNCH IS SERVED.

Then on to part two of our hike:

See the hollow in the base of the "Daniel Boone Tree". I call it this because D. Boone left record of his having spent a winter all snuggled up inside a tree much like this.

Cross over Snail Bridge, following the Old Wagon Trail that existed when this was a plantation. Can you make out, from the surrounding landscape, that this was once a wagon trail? What happened to the tracks from long ago? If we dug down in the earth here, what artifacts might we find?

Look for butterflies this afternoon. How is habitat loss causing their possible extinction?

Back along the wetlands bridge we go. Look for critter and varmint tracks along the mud and algae here. If an animal has hooves, is it likely to be a carnivore, omnivore, or herbivore?

Off the wetlands bridge and touch the Lucky Water Willow. Native Americans chewed this type of tree bark for painkiller. By the way, are there bacteria on everything you see? How do bacteria help us?

Up the hill. The clay dirt to your left – does it grow plants well? Why, or why not?

Enter the Black Forest, with virtually nothing but evergreen trees for the next five hundred yards (how many feet is that?). One full moon night, Mr. T. came upon some high school kids having a "pine cone fight" here. Why did they wear goggles?

What does the moon do to the ocean? Do you think it affects teenagers' brains too?

Now enter the Great Meadow. Imagine the Cherokee meeting here to play games. (Like we do today, they found that games were a much nicer substitute for war.) We will also play one. When Mr. T. says "Go", the contestants know what to do. Each class will have already chosen contestants (a boy and a girl) to race across the Great Meadow and give a gift pine cone to the tribe in the forest across the meadow. Name some ways that sports and games help us learn to be nicer to each other, even today.

Now sing "Follow the Ugly Gray Road" (because the upcoming path is made of concrete, not yellow brick). Notice the brilliant red leaves along this path.

We soon cast our gaze upon the Resting Tree, as it was called for longer than anyone alive now remembers.

But ... before you go further, leave all your laughing and silliness behind. This is a serene place, where you should show respect for the nameless slaves buried in unmarked graves.

You may gather some oak leaves, fallen from the Resting Tree, and place them on the graves, as a sign of respect. As you slip by, touch the tree, as you'll rarely in your lives ever lay your hands on anything that has lived for centuries, as has this tree.

What do you predict you'll like best about your hike? Make a top ten list here.

The Greatest of Games

(Dedicated to thefirsttee.org –

in honor and memory of my father, Don Talley)

I first learned how to play golf in a cornfield, a cow pasture, a backyard, and on a living room rug. Yet I went on to win five Tennessee state championships, receive a full golf scholarship to college, and earn All-American honors.

I also learned how to take a running leap over a barbed-wire fence quite well, too. Yes, indeed. Whenever I'd go over in the cow pasture to hit balls (used ones my dad had found at a local golf course) my hound dog would play a game. I don't know what he called it but I named it Chase the Bull Toward Ben. It's perhaps why I learned to play golf relatively fast, and not monstrously slow, as do too many.

Eventually, when some people began to notice that I had a special talent for golf (and not just barbed-wire fence leaping) Dad worked out a deal for me to play for free at a local course called Holston Valley. I would "work off" my greens fees … by raking leaves, mowing greens, whatever was needed.

So many wonderful adult-child friendships I formed at Holston Valley, and also at the local Steele Creek course. We couldn't afford the Bristol Country Club.

Dad taught me the about life through the game of golf. When I'd come home, he wouldn't ask what I shot. He'd ask, "Did you learn anything new about yourself today?" Or, "Were you nice to the people you played with?"

Dad always said you could learn all you ever needed to know about someone simply by playing a round of golf with them. "It doesn't matter what they score," said Dad. "Whether they shoot a 68 or 108, you'll know whether they play fair or cheat, whether they accept bad breaks or whine, and whether they easily give up or not."

All sports can teach us all of the above, it's true, but none can bare your soul to the bone and pull it off quite like Ye Grand Olde Game of Golf.

I can say this without a shred of doubt … if I could

have kids play just one sport today, it'd be golf. It might be the easiest way to a college athletic scholarship for many, especially for girls. And it's a sport everyone can play for the rest of their lives *with family*.

Later on in life, when I coached middle school golf, I'd drive around in a golf cart, continually carrying on a nonstop jovial banter with my players. It kept them from getting too nervous and brought a sense of fun to their play.

I only had two rules of coaching, rules that Dad had instilled within me long ago: Play hard and have fun.

Because of the way I often dressed - blue jeans (when I could get by with it at country clubs) and hiking boots - some parents and/or other coaches thought I didn't know a hill of beans about golf. Of course, I played right up to their perception by unleashing an onslaught of even more outlandish nonsense and buffoonery (again, things I learned from Dad).

I haven't played competitively at golf (or even played a friendly round with friends) in many, many years. Yet, even to this day, the contacts I made long ago (directly because of playing golf when young) have helped me raise hundreds of thousands of dollars for worthy children's causes in my hometown and region.

The First Tee organization is the most ingenious ever devised for allowing economically underprivileged children to be introduced to the game of golf … whether they be inner city kids of color, or poor white children of these hills. The First Tee is a youth development organization that builds character, instills life-enhancing values, and promotes making good life choices … all through the game of golf.

Worried about cost?

Don't.

Trust me and visit thefirsttee.org.

If you have a child or grandchild, you'll both forever treasure the day you introduced them to The Greatest of Games.

Amazing Grace

(Dedicated to: Big Brothers/Big Sisters of America, bbbs.org)

"Jake, do you know how I can tell you're lying?" I asked my little third grade friend.

"Nope", he grinned. (It seemed Jake forever kept an infectious grin pasted across his face, no matter what the occasion.)

I answered, "Your lips move."

Not everyone got it, of course. Only a few kids laughed. A few others told me that Jake had to move his lips to talk.

But Jake got it. He grinned at me again. If the eyes are truly windows to the soul, then Jake's baby blues told a horror story hidden within.

Jake's mouth may have been twisted into a perpetual grin, but his eyes reflected an ever-present, profound sadness. In a word, Jake's eyes were dim. In three words, they were dead fish eyes.

Jake's eyes leaped out as the main thing all perceptive children noticed about him, once they spent any time with Jake at all. His eyes were hollow, devoid of emotion.

"Nobody ever believes you, do they, Jake?" I asked.

"No, Mr. Talley, they don't, not even when I'm telling the truth. Everybody thinks I'm no good."

I had already told Jake about Aesop's timeless fable, The Boy Who Cried Wolf. The story fascinated him but met with no change in Jake's lying tendencies … or his cheating … or his stealing.

That these three vices often blossom within the same vase should come as no surprise, as they are practically one and the same.

The toxic combination of childhood lying, stealing and cheating, I've found, is virtually impossible for mere human intervention to stop once it gets a soul hold.

Now I'm not referring to the lying that all children do. All children lie (actually, given enough pressure and the "right" conditions, so do all adults . . . though many remain either too sanctimonious or psychologically ignorant of the fact to admit it).

Jake's lying was addictive, and often served no apparent purpose, unlike the vast majority of uttered untruths.

Jake had heard his mother lie countless times. I'd also heard her lie, right in front of Jake, more times than I care to recall.

Jake's father once found my wallet and returned it to me. He called Jake over with us and made a big deal out of it in front of him. He said proudly, with Jake standing there beside him, "This will show you, Jake, how to be honest".

Of course, Jake's father made mention of the fact that someone else had obviously gotten to my wallet before he found it, as all the money had already been taken out when he picked it up.

Little Jake knew what this meant ... his father was a liar and a thief, too.

We often wonder why our children don't appear to hear what we say. I think it's because they're so busy watching what we *do*. Our actions speak much louder than our words (whether we want them to or not).

"Jake," I told him one day, "you'd rather climb up and sit in a big briar bush and tell a lie than you would stand on plain ground and tell me the truth."

Jake grinned from ear to ear. But his eyes, as always, revealed the truth. Regardless of the opinion of many, Jake didn't really want to be this way.

I tried taking him places after school. His parents totally trusted me with Jake (and, besides that, it took him off their hands for a while).

Along with my son, who was very young at this time, I took to taking Jake on various fun activities and excursions.

We might go eat pizza. Or pass some baseball. Or gather some walnuts. Just anything to get Jake to see that there was "another lifestyle" beyond the only one he'd ever known.

Whenever I've sought to help a troubled child and that troublesome behavior remains, I'm sometimes asked the question, "Well, did it work?"

My answer is always the same. "I can't tell yet. They've got their whole life ahead of them."

Whenever I forgive a child again and again for doing something wrong, I'm sometimes told, "You're only making the kid worse by forgiving him so much without his behavior changing. You're spoiling him that way ... and no one can keep forgiving forever."

My answer is always the same. "Real forgiveness *is* forever and it's unconditional. Besides, we shouldn't expect to see a big behavior change right away because real forgiveness accomplishes things far into the future, things that we will likely never see."

People can be impatient. And if grace needs one thing above all ... it is time.

My intent is not to sound facetious. I simply mean to say that we often truly *can't* tell if our most earnest efforts have been rewarded. And I'm quite happy with that ... because it can serve to heighten our humility. I think if we could so easily tell when our good intentions are nourished, then we might grow much too proud. Humility is a powerful thing.

Not long after my becoming sort of a "big brother" to Jake, I caught him stealing from me in the lunchroom.

I went to pay my lunch bill and wondered aloud why it was so high.

The cafeteria manager told me, "Mr. Talley, you know it's where you've been rewarding Jake for being good. He told me how you were letting him charge an extra snack every day. I think that's a great idea, by the way. He's such a cute little – "

"Thief!" I interjected out loud, knowing full well I had never approved for Jake to charge food to my account.

I had to try something else . . . something really, really different.

"Jake," I said one morning, "Do you trust me?"

"Of course, Mr. Talley, I trust you more than anybody."

"Okay, then listen close, Jake. We're going to have a trial in class right after lunch. I want you to go last in line for lunch, so everybody will already be in the class when you go in. Then I want you to go into class a little ahead of me."

"Why?"

"Because I want you to take the twenty dollar bill I have in my top middle desk drawer. I want you to make a lot of noise when you open the drawer. Then stand there and hold the twenty dollar bill up until several of the kids can plainly see what you're doing. Then I want you to stick the money into your pocket and walk back to your desk. And whatever you do, don't say a word."

Jake didn't grin. And his hollow eyes only reflected confusion and hurt.

"It's okay, Jake. You're not really stealing, because I'm telling you to get it. But I want the other kids to *think* you're stealing the money, okay?"

"Why?"

"Because we're going to prove to everyone that there's good in you."

"How?"

"Just trust me, Jake, like I know you do. But you've got to promise not to tell anyone I said you could get the money, until I tell you to, or this won't work, okay?"

Jake didn't understand at all how this was going to work out for him. But trust me, he did. "Okay," he said.

Jake must have pulled off the caper flawlessly, because when I rounded the corner and entered the room I saw eyes popping and jaws dropping.

"Mr. Talley! Mr. Talley!" The little squealers chirped. There are always those, both young and old, who are eager to spill the beans on others. Most really didn't relish the thought of telling me, but some did.

"Let's hold a trial!" I announced. "No one can be found guilty in our country without a trial, can they?"

"But we all saw Jake," insisted many of my fellow little countrymen. "Do we really need to have a trial when so many witnesses saw exactly what happened?"

Wow! I realized then what a truly golden opportunity I'd created to show the judicial system of our great republic in action.

"Yes," I said. "We'll have a courtroom trial here and now." I knew we had the whole afternoon ahead of us, but I'd better act fast.

"Let's appoint a jury. But no one can sit on the jury who thinks they actually saw Jake take the money. Tell me why."

And they did.

Children will amaze you … if you clear all worksheets out of their way and let them think for themselves.

"Now tell me who would make the best prosecuting and defense attorneys. Who do you trust most in this class to be fair and just?"

Children will amaze you … if you let them create and improvise on their own, without always telling them exactly what they must learn.

The children voted on none other than the *exact* two classmates I'd have chosen myself, if I'd been voting alone.

I offered, "Should we be fairly sure, pretty sure, or almost certain, before we find the defendant guilty?"

There was some debate here (while Jake sat still all the while, trying not to cast nervous grins my way).

Finally, the class arrived at the consensus that they'd better be "pretty doggone sure" before they found Jake guilty.

"And what will be Jake's punishment, if found guilty?" I asked the class.

The children decided that the shame of all Jake's friends knowing was plenty punishment enough. And that maybe he could do some good deeds for our class as a way to help earn our trust back. That way, he'd feel better and not just get worse, which they all decided would surely happen if Jake were sent to the office. (Oh, if only an adult justice system could always be so wise.)

The trial commenced, with The Honorable Judge Talley presiding. (One of my mechanically inclined boys had quickly fashioned me a rather unique homemade gavel.)

Each witness was called, sworn in, examined, and cross-examined. It seems no matter how hard the defense tried, and they tried valiantly, there could be no apparent reason other than "theft" for Jake's actions.

Jake himself refused to take the stand, which the children learned to be his right. (Of course, later on, in retrospect, the children saw how this might have helped his case tremendously.)

The jury was nearly hung a time or two. At first, some kids just couldn't bring themselves to convict Jake, even though they "knew" he was guilty. After much heated discussion (the "noise" of democracy at work) a consensus was reached.

Jake was pronounced guilty as charged, of the crime of theft.

Not a single child stood and cheered at the verdict. Not even the squealers ... and not even the prosecuting attorney. The children had all done what they felt they had to do, but no one was particularly happy about it.

Everyone knew I must now pass sentence on Jake.

"Jake, please stand and face the court," I announced.

Jake looked at me, but he didn't utter a word. "I still trust you, Mr. Talley," his eyes said.

"Ladies and gentlemen of the jury," I said, "we've almost convicted an innocent friend."

After the gasps and murmurs subsided, I asked Jake, for all to hear, "Jake, did I tell you earlier today to take that twenty dollar bill from my desk?"

"Yes, sir."

"And if I told you to take it, then that can't be stealing, now can it?"

"No, sir."

Now instead of protesting about how I'd tricked them all into a trial, the children did another most amazing and honorable thing – they stood and cheered for Jake.

I think the prosecuting attorney was happiest of all. She even remarked how Jake's eyes seemed to light up the room.

Children will amaze you.

So will grace.

P. S. - I have a story about my "real" Little Brother (whom I was "matched" with by the local Big Brother-Big Sister organization). I would likely never have gone into teaching had we not met. More on that story in the upcoming second book of this series … The Real Appalachian America.

Spiritual Heart . . . Scientific Mind

(Are the people of Appalachia somehow more ignorant and uneducated than others? No, but all people are ... without science)

If the reader numbers among those courageous
individuals, always among the minority,
who relentlessly question authority . . .
I honor and dedicate the following words to you.
For without your light,
the masses would still burn witches by night,
guided by zealotry, superstition, and fright.
Indeed, without you –
those questioning, doubting, searching, fearless few –
a Dark Age we could yet so easily return to.

If one wishes not to doubt what one has been taught even a smidgen, or think for oneself as much as one iota, then one may not want to read farther in this chapter. Opening up one's mind to new knowledge can be disturbing, whether one be from Appalachia or Albuquerque.

As much as I love my region of America, I've found that one is likely to find no shortage of folks hereabouts who apparently know everything about the ultimate intentions of the Almighty.

However much we may claim to know about religion, some basic scientific literacy comes in handy for our understanding of the world ...and for enriching our spiritual lives.

And as one that daily seeks to nourish both a spiritual heart and a scientific mind, I feel particularly led to address the following commonly held misconceptions.

Therefore, I'd like to humbly offer a "top ten list" regarding scientific literacy, diluting popular misconception from reality.

10: Science and faith are in conflict with one another.

Reality: Faith deals with things spiritual. Science concerns itself only with the measurable, observable, physical world. The only conflict here is in the minds of people who choose to create a conflict. In reality, there is no conflict. As Galileo, the fearlessly inquisitive scientist and equally ardent man of faith, so aptly put it, "Scripture tells us how to go to heaven. Science tells us how the heavens go."

9: People should be fearful of science.

Reality: Many people are fearful when their cherished, long-held beliefs are challenged. Science is only interested in one thing – the truth about the physical universe in which we live. The only folks who need to fear science are those who think they already know the truth, the whole truth, and nothing but the truth. (If you claim to have total knowledge about anything, then you probably should fear science . . . and fear it very, very much.)

8: If you believe in evolution, you're headed straight for a visit with the devil (whose beak probably resembles one of Charles Darwin's famous finches).

Reality: Evolution is not a "belief" system. Therefore, it has absolutely nothing to do with religion in any way. Evolution and natural selection are widely accepted by the vast majority of educated people worldwide. As far as scientific proof, they rank right up there alongside the Earth revolving around the sun. There's enormous evidence for both. Nothing in all of modern biology and genetics makes a shred of sense without evolution. The fact that "things change over time" in the world is agreed upon by every reasonable person virtually anywhere on the planet. That is . . . until you give this fact that "things change over time" a certain name that begins with the letter e.

7: Aliens have visited the Earth, with evidence hidden by a massive government cover-up.

Reality: We almost certainly are not alone in this vast universe, but neither have we been visited by little green men. Far weirder than aliens, do you realize that we appear to be nearing evidence that our universe itself is not alone, that there are an infinite number of parallel universes, in countless numbers of which carbon copies of you and I also exist? Don't laugh too hard. For a long time, imagining a spherical (round) Earth once seemed just as weird.

6: Global warming (more properly called global climate change) is a big lie put out there by them tree-huggin' hippies.

Reality: Global climate change is now widely accepted as very real (and largely human induced) by virtually all reputable scientists and educated people the planet over, be they liberal, conservative, or independent. The Earth's climate knows no politics.

5: Humans are the ultimate species. (Actually, cats appear to think they are.)

Reality: We humans are already on our way toward becoming cyborgs (part human, part machine). It's coming, whether we like it or not. Even more striking – we humans may inevitably be able to transfer an exact digital blueprint of our minds into a computer or robot, achieving a strange (and somewhat frightening) sort of immortality. And just when we thought the economy was big news.

4: Science is hard to understand.

Reality: Scientists do experiments and/or record observations. That's it. They strive to make each experiment and/or observation as "repeatable" as possible (so that all other scientists in the world following exactly the same procedure are able to either verify or nullify the results) if a new truth is purported to be discovered. In fact, scientists try very hard to *disprove* each other. Scientists the world over try and try again, often taking many years, to disprove new discoveries that appear to be true. If years of controlled experiments and/or repeated observations ultimately *can't* disprove the results – then a new truth may be claimed as discovered . . . but not before.

3: Time slows down for no one.

Reality: According to one of Albert Einstein's imminently verified equations, it actually can very nearly stop. Nearing light speed, we could live for eons, as compared to time passing for our friends on Earth.

2: One person can't change the world.

Reality: Yes, we can . . . and we do. According to quantum physics, and apparently verified by nearly eighty years of countless laboratory experiments, it appears we change *the entire universe forever* (and/or quite possibly even create a new, parallel one) with our every little thought and action. (So kiss a big ol' fat 'goodbye' to ever thinking you're not important anymore.)

1: Science tries to disprove God's existence.

Reality: Science can neither prove, nor disprove, the existence of God. Nor does it attempt to do so. God is very much alive and well within the realm of faith . . . and appears to be quite happy with keeping it that way.

Finding the Real Santa Claus

(Dedicated to the Bristol Public Library)

Years ago I bought the best Santa suit I could find. I still have the suit. The only difference is that now I don't need to use a pillow for a fake belly anymore.

I've got that covered.

Playing jolly old St. Nicholas at elementary school has proven to be one of my life's greatest joys.

During my initial rounds down the school hallway to the pre-school room I find one hundred percent true believers.

I've learned to come in quickly with a big "Ho! Ho! Ho!" to disarm the wee tykes. I find if I come in too slowly their fears and doubts actually increase. St. Nick must be lively and quick.

Alas, the tiniest hint of apostasy begins in kindergarten, although it's probably the most fun place to visit. The children are more animated and actually want to talk to me and hug me a bit. I suppose, by this age, they've been pushed forward enough times to sit on the lap of a big weird guy they've never met (think of how frightening the standard visit with Santa must be to smaller children).

As I sling my sack of toys over my back and prepare to scamper out the door, one kid will invariably call out, "Are you Mr. Talley?"

My cover in dire danger of being blown, I say something akin to, "Mr. Talley sure looks and acts a lot like me, doesn't he? He's a good friend of mine. Tell Mr. Talley you saw me if you see him today, okay?"

That usually satisfies the inquisitive little cherubs, at least until I make my getaway to first grade.

There the children who believe I'm the real Santa number around eighty percent. As an extra precaution, I lower my voice and change the inflection a bit.

These kids are savvy to the slightest hint of an imposter, especially if they've been around me as a teacher at their school for any amount of time. Many of these children have older brothers and sisters whom I've taught, so they do tend to catch a clue or two as to who Santa might "really" be.

By the time Santa rolls into second grade, his cover is almost one hundred percent blown. Most of the kids remember me from prior yearly visits, so they just grin and yell, "It's Mr. Talley!"

I don't mind ... and neither do they.

We all feel that a visit from St. Nick, real or pretend, is still a worthy venture for us all.

For many years my third, fourth, and fifth grade students actually received a Christmas Eve call from the Jolly Old Elf himself. Santa would "Ho! Ho! Ho!" into the phone and tell each child that he was bringing them a lump of coal . . . or if they had brothers or sisters – two lumps for each of them.

By this age much of the magic is gone, but enough of a flicker remains to enjoy a call from a friendly trickster.

Early one Christmas morning, just on a lark (as a British St. Nick might say), I threw on my Santa suit and drove down to the Bristol Jail.

My Santa attire is so authentic (beard, hair, boots, belt, toy sack and all) that I should have called ahead. One of the deputies thought I was a drunkard leftover from the previous night's festivities. He nearly wouldn't let me in the back door. Finally he got close enough to recognize my voice.

The deputies at the Bristol Jail are some of our city's finest men and women. They go out their way to get me in to see the male inmates whenever they can (and sometimes when they can't). Excellence travels from the sheriff on down, as Bristol has long been blessed with some of the brightest and most compassionate beings I've ever known in law enforcement.

With some in such a position, of course, the power trip does go to their head, but not with our sheriff or the vast majority of his deputies.

Santa was welcomed in to visit the cell blocks that Christmas morning.

The inmates slapped me all manner of high and low fives as I breezed by their cells. It was early, but even those still in bed rose up eagerly to greet me. One cell block even clapped and cheered.

Driving home (still fully dressed in proper attire) I thought about my jaunt through the jail. I began to believe that the magic of St. Nicholas never really completely dies within us, no matter how old or cynical we may grow.

Maybe the giving spirit of St. Nicholas is at once both fictional and real. Perhaps he largely exists as a reality within us all, should we desire to find him.

Shedding Light on Monsters

(Dedicated to The Children's Advocacy Center of Bristol/Washington County and our local CASA – Court Appointed Special Advocates for children)

In the minds of children, monsters can be real.

Since monsters seem to like shadows, I tell children that monsters are afraid of light.

Science sheds light on monsters, proving whether or not they're real. I've told my students this many a time, as this truth often piques their natural-born interest in how science enlightens our minds … and drives away needless fear and superstition.

Among many adults, the general consensus is often to just *tell* children that monsters aren't real and let it go at that.

I'm not sure that's the best way … especially with some monsters.

Many a science lesson my young students and I have spent together, using the wonderful experiential thought processes integral to employing one of humanity's greatest inventions; the Scientific Method. This wonderful creation of reason and experiment allows anyone with an open mind to deduce, induce, and/or infer as to the validity of various purported truths, myths, monsters, and/or urban legends.

For children, among the most notable of such are: Bigfoot, The Loch Ness Monster, Freddy Krueger, ghosts, vampires, alien conspiracy theories, and the world ending any moment now.

But regardless of the obvious nonexistence of werewolves when the moon is full, there do indeed exist things in this world that are even more horrendous … yet just as real as any shadow.

These things will not be explicitly detailed within this writing, as I realize these contents will be made available to children.

Yet let it be said that I have at least thrice come face-to-face with real monsters in my hometown … monsters perhaps more demonic … and certainly much more real … than the devils of our worst nightmares.

These three confrontations are the only times I've ever felt like killing another human being, due to what these monsters perpetrated upon the lives of the defenseless innocent.

I will tell of two of those encounters here. The third has been presented in an earlier chapter. (I use the term "monster" because, if you were to ask the victims, the description fits.)

At the jail, a mistake was made.

I was sitting alone in the library, waiting for one of the deputies to bring me an inmate who was interested in obtaining his GED. This deputy had inadvertently failed to tell me that this young man had been placed in a cell isolated from the inmate population. Nor was I told that this inmate had brutally raped and murdered a girl whom I'd taught only a few years before.

The library door locked shut.

Less than a minute into my interview I realized the deputy had made a terrible mistake. One mistake almost compounded into two when I heard the man snicker about his crime beneath his breath. To this day I don't know how he got out of the library with his head still attached to the rest of his body. We were both blessed, I suppose, that another deputy just happened by to open the door the very instant my blood was ready to boil.

Another time I nearly took the law into my own hands.

A different little girl, a student of mine at the time, pleaded for me to "make my uncle stop". By the look on her face, I knew exactly what she meant. This was my first year teaching and I didn't think as clearly as I might have today. Primal emotion can do that to us, even to the calmest of us.

That afternoon, when school let out, I took a two-iron (golf club) and walked up the sidewalk into the front door of her apartment (I didn't knock).

By the grace of heaven (somehow thrown toward the both of us) the monster had been looking out the window at that very moment (probably because his helpless niece was due to arrive home on the bus). He had seen me coming.

If he caught the look etched on my face as I approached up the sidewalk, I have no doubt why he ran out the back door and (literally) left the state later that same day. He never returned to our good town, so far as I ever heard.

Monsters are afraid of light.

These may seem strange occurrences, coming from someone of my nonviolent Quaker beliefs, but, again – when emotion floods the most ancient reptilian part of our brain, it can lead people to act in ways we normally wouldn't.

And nothing stirs our instinctive, collective anger quite like seeing a child being abused. From my teaching at the jail, I've found that even the most hardened drug dealers and thieves, who share a crude code of honor amongst themselves, share nothing but rage and disgust toward those who harm children in such a way.

But once one is a monster, is one always a monster? I understand that the recidivism (backsliding) rate is very high for child molesters and abusers ... and even one percent is far too much to accept.

Yet ... that Light deep within my soul tells me these people are people, too, more like us all than not.

I'm sure there are many things that I don't know about these people. Did they once suffer as victims of indescribably horrible happenings in their own lives?

But then, not every victim is doomed to become a victimizer. Some of the gentlest, kindest, and spiritually strongest people I know were themselves victims of childhood atrocities. From the sourest of sour lemons these battered souls persevered to create the sweetest lemonade.

Why are there no monuments built to honor such people ... the victims who return such childhood violence with nothing but kindness toward everyone they meet thereafter?

Perhaps our greatest hope for prevention lies not in the rehabilitation of abusers, but in education of the masses. The fact that the reader finds me facing down this topic in print speaks hope to our culture, that we will no longer ignore early warning signs or pretend "out of sight, out of mind".

Certainly, from my experience with the men at the jail, I find that an alarming number hint or whisper to me of having suffered a similar fate as children, though none will announce it for all to hear. I find the topic to be strong taboo amongst virtually all grown men, in jail or not.

I read where the Balinese islanders (some would say a culture "inferior" to our own) consider children to be sacred beings. I think most of us would agree that if anything in our world is to be held sacred, it should be childhood.

Whether they be goblins, gremlins, or ghouls, all children will experience their monsters of some sort. As adults, we share a mutual responsibility to shine the light of science and reason toward them all ... before any become real.

Jumping into Holes

(Dedicated to the Boys and Girls Club of Bristol)

Sam spent more time over the course of a day figuring out how to get into trouble than he spent in a whole year opening books.

Sam had been getting into trouble for so long that it had come to be part of his everyday life. He told me, "I feel kinda bad if I don't get into at least a little bit of trouble durin' the day. I feel like I ain't accomplishin' nothin'".

Sam's personable good-nature had a way of toning down his trouble-making aggravations, at least with most folk.

But there's always one teacher (every school has at least one, and some are endowed with one at each grade level) who deems themselves as The One Who Must Be Obeyed.

In that particular school, that would be Ms. D.

Ms. D. saw it as her divinely called duty to put Sam and his like "in their place". She had taught Sam for two straight years before he promoted to my grade. It was two straight years because she had somehow talked the principal into holding Sam back a year, after she'd had him once, just so she could "put him more into his place".

It didn't work … either year.

On a good day, Ms. D. just screamed and shouted at her students. On bad days she growled and howled. On really bad days, she shrieked and screeched … and growled and howled.

But Sam got special treatment. Ms. D. punished that poor boy every which way her mind could possibly conjure up.

Sam told me at the first of his year with me, "I reckon Ms. D.'s gonna sleep better this year."

"How's that, Sam?"

"Cause that poor old withered-up thing won't have to lay awake every night thinkin' all about how she's gonna put me in my place the next day."

I don't see how anyone could not like Sam … in trouble or not.

Sam was now out of Ms. D.'s classroom for good. But that hardly slowed him down from giving her trouble when ever he could.

Once I sent him on an errand to the principal's office. On the way, he stuck his head into her classroom door, and loudly commented, "Ms. D., I do believe you've lost some weight this year!"

Everyone knew what to expect next. There began a low, slowly rising, guttural growl, emanating from Ms. D. Once the growl reached a crescendo, she stomped over to Sam and started walking him toward the office.

"That's mighty kind of you, Ms. D. I was just headed that way myself." The lady just couldn't seem to squash Sam's sense of fun, no matter how hard she tried.

Sam just wouldn't be "put into place".

Once, as we walked down the hallway, my class was passing by Ms. D.'s. You would hardly know Ms. D.'s class ever walked the hall way if you didn't see them. No child dared intentionally produce even the feeblest peep, for fear of initiating the guttural growl response.

But Sam decided to be himself.

"Ms. D., your class just ain't the same without me, now, is it? Don't you just wish you had me back?"

Think "low, guttural growl" initiating now.

Another time I heard the guttural growl emanating from just outside my door. I had just allowed Sam to go to the bathroom, so I didn't have to wonder who might be the intended recipient of the growl's sound waves.

When I looked out in the hall, Ms. D. had Sam cornered into a little nook.

Ms. D. continued growling (with obvious immense pleasure) toward Sam that he should now turn and tell me exactly what he was just now doing in the hall.

Sam replied, "I was just cleanin' the hallway wall, Mr. T. It's got to be done in the proper fashion. Watch!" Sam resumed his previous activity of leaning over and sliding his whole arm against the smooth concrete hall wall, while walking alongside (which is actually quite a common method of walking hallways for many a hyperactive elementary boy – I can even recall doing so myself in my own youth).

At Sam's resuming of his previous activity, the gutter grumbled forth a particularly turbulent rumble. I do believe I could nearly see it vibrate the very air we breathed.

"Grumble, grumble, roil and rumble!" (With all due apologies to the witches of Shakespeare's *Macbeth*.)

I had to rescue Sam.

The rumble had risen to a verified roar by the time I reached him.

"Young man, you are making too much noise in this hallway!" blared forth Ms. D. like a trumpet. *"Your loud noise is disturbing all the other classes in this hallway!"*

Sam stopped, looked around at Ms. D. and said, "Ms. D., I don't mean to sound disrespectful and all, but ain't you bein' a whole lot louder than me right about now?"

The gutter went silent. Sam was the only kid who could ever stop it speechless, at least for a few seconds now and then.

It was my chance to step in. "Sam, I'd like to ask you to apologize to Ms. D."

So Sam did.

"He doesn't mean a word of it!" growled Ms. D.

Actually, I don't think Ms. D. would have accepted Sam's apology had he handed to her written in his own blood. Her mind was long ago made up … and sealed tighter than the scowl on her face.

Later that day, at lunch, I asked Sam why he gave me so little trouble and Ms. D. so much.

"Because she asks for it and you don't."

"What do you mean by that?"

Sam swallowed a bite and paused before explaining. Little did I realize it would be the most unusual and profound description of teaching that I would ever hear from anyone.

"It's like this, Mr. T. If I was to fall into a big hole in the ground, so to speak, most teachers would come over and tell you how to get out. They wouldn't forget about you. Teachers are good people. They'd stand up there and keep yellin' at you again and again about what you should do, just like Ms. D. would do, whether you were getting' out of the hole or not. Most kids would get out this way, but some just wouldn't ever make it."

Sam continued.

"Now what I'd call the really good teachers would come over and stoop down to give you a hand. They'd actually do their part to help you out of the big hole. But if you still couldn't get out, they'd keep reachin' down anyway, some of 'em for a mighty long time before they gave up on you."

Sam had my rapt attention.

"Now there are a few teachers, a very few, who would look at the situation and do somethin' completely different, somethin' that might even hurt them a bit or even get them into some trouble."

"What?" I could barely wait to hear Sam's answer.

"They'd jump down into the hole with you."

There was a pause before I asked, "Then what?"

"Then you'd both figure a way to get out of the hole together."

I didn't have to ask Sam which type of teacher would best help him find his place.

. . .

Sam's mischievous penchant for trouble-making followed him on through school. It had become too much a part of who he was for him to ever completely stop.

Today he's leading a productive, meaningful, and quite happy life, along with his wife and three young children.

And his children are lucky to have such a good and courageous father. They say the apple doesn't fall far from the tree, so a crystal ball isn't needed to see whether they'll be getting into at least a little bit of trouble in school someday.

It's probably a good thing Ms. D. went ahead and retired before they come her way.

Which reminds me … I wonder if Sam's going to teach his little urchins how to clean a school hallway wall in the proper fashion?

I surely hope so …

Hope for Joe and Sue

(Dedicated to all who support adult literacy/education for the homeless, the destitute, and the incarcerated … any place on Earth where they may be found)

Imagine Joe and Sue. It isn't hard to do.

Joe is a real person, having attended Bristol Public Schools. He's a homegrown Bristolian.

Joe is only twenty, but he's been incarcerated, on and off, since age thirteen.

From juvenile detention to adult jail, Joe has graduated up the ladder of crime. He's even done a stint in prison.

Joe is a ninth-grade dropout, with no family resources, no money, and no place to call home.

One might say that Joe has no hope and be plainly stating the truth.

If Joe goes the way of so many who've walked in his shoes, he will live off you and me for the remaining half century or so of his life. Whether as an incarcerated inmate, or as a poor honest man on welfare, Joe will force you and me to pay dearly because he now sees himself as having no hope.

Yet … maybe there is some hope for Joe.

Yes, indeed, thanks to adult education provided at a net cost of *pennies a year per inmate* in the Bristol Jail, Joe has some hope.

Oh, I might as well skip ahead a bit and tell you that Joe has already taken advantage of his chance. He earned his GED (often referred to as a high school equivalency diploma) while incarcerated at Bristol Jail.

It's true a GED is not a college degree, but it is the absolute minimum educational requirement needed to go on to college … or to apply for any meaningful job in America today.

Indeed, not only is Joe now working every day at a meaningful job, he is also trying to be a father to his expectant first child.

Allow me to introduce you to Sue.

Sue is the pregnant mother of Joe's child. They plan to marry soon.

The stability of Joe's job even allows his future wife to continue her education, with hopes of becoming a nurse.

Sue, also a former inmate now on probation, graduated high school by the skin of her teeth. Many may have seen her walking the streets of downtown Bristol late of the evening, before she became pregnant with Joe's child.

By the way, I taught Sue in third grade. She was once an intellectually promising student, though almost no one in the last few years of her life would have believed it.

Money loaned or granted to Sue (ultimately from you and me, as taxpayers) to attend college is wisely invested. She has an unusual sense of urgency to succeed, maybe even more so than the typical college student.

Because Sue now has hope.

Joe and Sue have both begun attending local counseling sessions, an event which has also guided them toward good neonatal care for their unborn child. Indeed, they are trying to create a better future for their soon-to-be baby (who otherwise would almost certainly continue the cycle of crime and poverty inherited from his/her parents and their current environment).

Several of the community service agencies listed in this book are now helping guide Joe and Sue toward a better life for them and - especially - for their child.

It may even be possible to estimate the financial benefit to society derived from Joe and Sue returning to the workforce as tax-payers, as opposed to others who become lifelong tax-takers.

As of this writing, I've taught no less than three hundred and thirty-two inmates who have earned their GED while incarcerated in the Bristol Jail over the years.

If an inmate stays incarcerated (however much we may feel able to morally or socially "justify" that he or she deserves it), such incarceration costs us taxpayers many thousands of dollars a year ... just to keep him/her behind bars. Estimates vary widely, but you can be certain the cost will swell into the hundreds of thousands for those with longer sentences.

Of course, when an inmate is returned to society and finds a decent job, he may become a lifetime tax-payer, as opposed to a lifetime tax-taker. Society's benefit from such a metamorphosis is probably immeasurable over the lifetime of a young man (or woman) whose life is redirected.

In reality, the "real life" cost for a single uneducated young inmate who returns to the street jobless (and hopeless), as opposed to one who has obtained their GED and is able to return to society and keep a meaningful job, may well number close to half a million dollars.

And that's just for one life.

Admittedly, such an estimate is probably low, especially if the individual is young, keeps a job, and stays out of the penal system.

However many millions we may ultimately save ourselves in tax dollars, none of these estimates takes into account the most valuable benefit of all – that of an inmate reconnecting with his/her family. That outcome is surely incalculable by any statistical measure, but undeniably invaluable toward bettering our society as a whole.

We hold behind bars a larger percentage of our populace than any other democracy on Earth. Closing in on eight million of us (no, that's not a misprint … that's approximately one of every thirty-one adults in America) currently languish in prison, in jail, on probation, or on parole.

Passing the blame after the fact helps little.

Solving problems before they come to happen helps a lot.

In Charles Dickens' classic, *A Christmas Carol*, he warns us what humanity should fear most. At one spirit's visit, Scrooge turns his head and begs that he does not wish to look upon the children of Want and Ignorance anymore.

The spirit complies, but wisely counters with, "They're still there."

(Indeed, when a parent goes to jail, please rest very well assured, their children are sentenced right along with them – whether we choose to see this or not.)

We don't need to go "soft" on hard crime. I realize, most certainly from personal experience, that some inmates are so misdirected, and their crimes so horrific, that their chances of ever contributing meaningfully to society are virtually impossible.

However, for the vast majority of inmates, the Joe's and Sue's of our world, there is hope (if we offer it to them) of returning to society as a working citizen, contributing to our community.

As it presently stands, our penal system might as well hang the sign from Dante's Inferno (which hung over the entrance to hell) over the entrance to each and every penal institution in America. The foreboding sign read, "Abandon all hope, ye who enter here."

Indeed, we need to give hope to these people.

Hope and education and a chance to work; they are the keys to a better life, for them … for us all.

This is not an impossible thing to do. All it takes is a turnaround in public attitude, from punitive to rehabilitative.

In the words of a great song from my youth, "You may say I'm a dreamer, but I'm not the only one."

A Good Dam Sleigh Ride

(Dedicated to Healing Hands Health Center, Crossroads Medical
Mission, and RAM – Remote Are Medical … all are wonderful non-
profit groups who provide
free health care for Appalachian residents)

No explanation is deemed necessary. The title speaks
for itself.

Sugar Hollow Dam in Bristol, Virginia is capable of
providing our citizens with some of the best sleigh-
riding times you'll ever hang a memory on.

The most memorable time for me, as is often the case
with life's most exhilarating events, was my first.

My son was only six. The dam was vacant on a snowy
night, an unusual sight. Usually teenagers from local high
schools flock in droves to adorn its crest and slopes in
such weather.

Perhaps no one else came this night because the back
of the dam, where the best sledding takes place, was
covered with a thin sheet of ice.

Perhaps it was because the chill factor was near
ten degrees Fahrenheit.

Perhaps it was because my son and I went after
nine-o'clock on a school night.

Regardless, my young son and I had the whole dam to
ourselves. I brought my old Silver Streak sled, a relic of the
Sixties. For icy slopes it was better than the saucer type
sled we normally used for softer snow.

Lo and behold, on our first run we went clear to the
creek! David, who held tightly to my back, said "Dad, I
think I hear ice cracking."

He was right.

I sat up and stepped gingerly out onto thin ice, promptly
falling right through up to my knees, drenched below by
the liquid form of H2O.

David sat snugly on the sled and cackled at my predicament like a little rooster, until I threatened to introduce his feathers to the creek.

Of course, sleigh riding down such a large dam can be dangerous. But over the years, there have been relatively few serious injuries, proof that people can have a ton of thrilling fun and practice safety, too.

Every two-legged creature who's experienced such a thrill would surely agree with me ... to have a ton of fun on a snowy night you should go enjoy a good dam sleigh ride at Sugar Hollow Park.

Nothing Could Be More

(as told by son David, at age 5)

(Dedicated to all those parents who give their children time
and attention . . . more so than money and things)

It was late in the month of February. A snowfall came.
Dad and I walked up to the dam at Steele Creek. We had
parked at Rooster Front Park. I told Dad the night was so
white it was dark.

We could hardly hear our own footsteps. Dad says we
have to be quiet to see a great horned owl.

To help me keep quiet I pretended a big T. Rex was
asleep in the snow on top of the dam. If I made a noise he
would wake up and eat me.

I didn't make a sound. Dad even worried that I wasn't
breathing.

On top of the dam we first heard him.

No, not the T. Rex.

"Hoo! Hoo! Hootey-hoo!"

It was an owl!

He sounded to me as big as an evergreen tree. I could
see lots of big evergreens wearing snow by the lakeside.

We walked real soft through the snow straight toward
the sound. The hoot came from somewhere way up a steep
slope.

We stopped right beneath a big tree. But this tree
wasn't an evergreen. It had no leaves.

The full moon peeped straight down through the middle
of the big naked tree.

Dad called out for the owl, "Hoo! Hoo! Hootey-hoo!"
We heard nothing. We saw not anything.

I was really still and quiet. I kept looking up all around
and holding my breath.

Dad called out again, "Hoo! Hoo! Hootey-hoo!"
We heard and saw nothing again.

Then, there he was. High up and straight above my head, perched on a limb, there was the great horned owl!

Even better than that, the moon looked like it was right behind him. The owl and the moon looked to me to be so close that I could reach right up and touch them both.

Later I told Dad seeing the owl against the moon was better than magic.

But right then Dad and I dared not say a word to each other. Neither did we move a muscle.

I wondered why I hadn't heard the owl land. Nothing can hear him fly! Dad told me later that his feathers are made so his food can't hear him coming.

The owl looked down at Dad and me. He seemed to look at us both for a good long while. But I felt especially that he was looking at me.

The three of us stood stiller than the snow all around us.

Then, as suddenly as he came, the owl was gone.

I didn't even see him leave. I glanced away once for about half a second to look at Dad, then looked back up at the owl. But he had already leaped off the limb and flown away.

We stared up at the limb where the owl had stood against the moon. Nothing was moving anywhere, except falling snowflakes.

Neither did we move, for I don't know how long. It seemed to me like Dad wanted to see more.

But I don't know why. Because I felt like nothing could be more than what we saw.

Our Storytelling Culture

(In honor of Beaver Creek Storytellers of Bristol and the
International Storytelling Center of Jonesborough, Tn)

In these here hills, we cherish a good story. We talk in
stories. We sing in stories. Heck, we even think in stories.
Stories are important to us Appalachian folk, whether
those stories be fact or fiction. In fact, it may come as a
paradox to some, but it's the fictional stories that are often
the best ... especially for telling the truth.
Just ask children.

I especially like what one fifth-grade boy once said
to me when I told him that Jesus' parables were not true
in the literal sense, nor were they intended to be. I
related how these great stories were "just made up" so
that we could understand a deeper truth more clearly
than if Jesus had only stated dry, uninspiring facts.

The boy thoughtfully mused for a moment, then said, "I
get it now. If Jesus had said, 'You all be good', it wouldn't
have taught us very much. And even worse, we might not
even remember anything he said. That's why I like that old
Greek fable, Androcles and the Lion. It teaches kids that
kindness always comes back to you in a good way some
day. Plus we never forget the story, once we've heard it."

This inquisitive, bright young soul was already
well along his path toward seeking the deeper meaning
of things, a path too many adults fear to tread.

Indeed, let me count the ways; since the dawn of
human culture - parables, myths, sagas, ballads, tall tales,
allegories, fantasies, and fables – all have often enjoyed
far greater success at revealing humanity's deeper, more
meaningful truths than "just the facts, ma'am".

Planting Children . . . A Way of Life

(Dedicated to the Bristol Chamber of Commerce)

Besides painting a portrait kind and true of the remarkable people of the Appalachian region, one of the missions of this book is to inspire people (educators, parents, caregivers, etc.) to instill within children a lifetime appreciation for community service and a love for the natural world. Such a mission is conducted on the premise that it's difficult for anyone to love stars, streams, and butterflies ... and not also become more empathetic and loving toward our fellow human beings.

Planting Children (the name I've given my own little "way of life" business) strives to accomplish this mission by the conducting of personally guided nature hikes and day camps, during the summer and on various Saturdays throughout the school year. Our focus is geared directly toward Bristol's elementary-age schoolchildren, but any child aged kindergarten-12th grade may participate.

Local high school-age volunteers often help the Camp Director (yours truly) guide younger children at our Nature Camps, thereby earning community service hours (as pre-approved by local high schools) which may be used to bolster their college application resumes. In fact, our local community college, Virginia Highlands Community College, even accepts the hours that a high school student spends helping at Planting Children toward fulfilling part of an agreement for that student to attend their college tuition free for two full years.

We also hope to develop partnerships with the student teaching directors of local colleges, allowing future educators the opportunity to see our work in action, thereby opening their minds to alternative teaching methods.

A long-range goal/hope of Planting Children is to provide college scholarship opportunities for qualified youth applicants who, as a result of their chosen career path, are committed toward making a better world for us all.

Planting Children works jointly in open partnership with others to better enhance the lives of local children in our community.

No child ever pays to participate in any of our hikes, camps, events, or community service functions. Many good people in our local community help support us to make all this possible. To those supporters we are deeply grateful. Through Planting Children, local children have planted thousands of trees, cleaned countless acres of trash, and created many miles of hiking trails for public use. We strive to instill within each child the lifelong desire to give back to their community … as a way of life.

We hope that the reader will inspire others to do the same.

If the reader would like to donate to our various causes and endeavors for needy local children, you may mail a check to: Planting Children, P.O. Box 861, Bristol, VA 24203.

On behalf of the children of our entire region … thank you!

Planting Seeds of Hope

(Dedicated to the people of Bristol, and the entire Appalachian region, who make it such a good place to live)

I read a parable of how a man had changed the world.

It happened over a period of some thirty years, simply by his planting seeds daily.

The book, *The Man Who Planted Trees,* by French author Jean Giono, is brief but potentially life-changing. One cannot read it without being inspired in some sense.

I was inspired to embark upon somewhat of the same mission as did the book's humble main character, albeit on a smaller scale.

At first, I thought only "literally", as do many along the first steps of a spiritual journey.

The children and I began by literally planting acorns … thousands and thousands of them.

As related to earlier in the Resting Tree chapter, a countless lineage of the great oak's children was widely dispersed to other ground, due to my students and I having snuggled thousands of her acorns down into the Appalachian soil each autumn. Who knows how many little Resting Trees now reach for the sun around our town and region?

Also, since the beginning of our efforts, the children of our entire region have endeavored to plant young seedling trees of an innumerable variety.

Thanks to the generosity of donors, approximately six thousand local elementary-aged children have been able to plant tens of thousands of seedling trees over the years. Most of these were planted at children's homes and named in honor of family loved ones, thereby increasing their chances of personal care … and ultimate survival.

The children and I have also planted seedlings on recently logged national forest land. And we even have plans to plant young American chestnut trees on restored strip mine acreage in the near future.

I know of no bounds to the good that can be accomplished by a child planting a tree.

To begin with, simply observing the imprint of meaningful joy etching its way across a child's face is worth perhaps even more than the tree.

Over its lifetime, a single tree not only consumes carbon, but can potentially produce thousands of tons of oxygen to help nourish the planet.

And beyond all that … trees just downright beautify our community and our world.

Little by little, as I moved further along my spiritual path, I learned not to be so literally limited about planting seeds … or trees.

I got the idea that one might nourish the world at least as well by planting seeds and trees of a totally different sort.

My primary seeds would not be acorns or seedlings, but the hopes and dreams of children instead. I would nourish these seeds by my daily making the most personalized and positive influence I could conceive to be possible within the lives of children and their families.

I also sought to plant seeds and trees in a few other ways.

One would be by personalized, just-drop-by, weekly home visits to my students.

Another would be by writing several personalized notes daily.

Yet another would be by introducing children to Nature, allowing them to develop a passionate and lasting love for wild things. I resolved to take many a child on a hike over the years, as I knew that teaching children to love the wild works wonders for creating a more peaceable world.

Particularly, I sought to plant seeds of hope and light where I found them the least, within the families and children of the jail inmates I taught … and the homeless I visited.

It's a fact that we all plant seeds of some sort, whether we know it or not. Will the reader join me in planting seeds mindfully around our own communities, perhaps with a renewed passion?

What more meaningful act could one do - in one's brief time on this planet - than to voluntarily help better the lives of others?

Volunteering our time and energy to humbly help others numbers among the most immeasurably powerful things we can do – and we are limited only by our spirits, not by our bank accounts or social status.

If one wishes, one can easily find many worthy local civic clubs and volunteer organizations merely by doing an Internet search.

So … what cause stirs your soul? May your search yield for you a wonderful journey … and thanks for joining me on our journey together through these pages, through the heart and soul of the real Appalachian America.

Ben Talley

Made in USA - Kendallville, IN
1208824_9781717812353
12.11.2020 1250